Contents

Reading is one of the fastest ways for you to get information. *Reading Math* can help you improve the way you read and understand math topics. You will also learn how to improve your test-taking skills.

Before You Read

These steps can help you *preview* an article and get an idea of what it is about.

Read the title. Ask yourself "What can I learn from the title?" and "What do I already know about this subject?"

Read the first sentence or two. The writer wants to catch your attention in the first sentence or two. You may also find out what you are about to learn.

Skim the entire article. Look over the article quickly for words that may help you understand it. Jot down unfamiliar words in your Personal Dictionary. You can ask someone later what they mean.

Participate in class discussions. Your teacher may show you pictures or objects and ask you questions about them. Try to answer the questions.

While You Read

Here are some tips to help you make sense of what you read:

Concentrate. If your mind wanders, remind yourself of what you learned when you previewed the article.

Ask yourself questions. Ask yourself "What does this mean?" or "How can I use this information?"

Look for the topic of each paragraph. Each paragraph has a main idea. The other sentences build on that idea. Find all of the main ideas to understand the entire article.

Refer to the vocabulary you have learned. The words in dark type will remind you of what you learned in the Vocabulary section. For more help, refer to the previous page.

After You Read

The activities in *Reading Math* will help you practice different ways to learn.

A. Organizing Ideas Webs, charts, and tables will help you organize information from the article. Sometimes you will create art or apply math skills.

B. Comprehension Skills will help you recall facts and understand ideas.

C. Reading Strategies will suggest ways to make sense of what you read.

D. Expanding Vocabulary will teach you more about the vocabulary you learned before and during reading.

Vocabulary Assessment

After every five lessons, you can try out what you have learned. Activities, such as postcards and advertisements, show you how the vocabulary can be useful and fun in everyday life. Enjoy!

JAMESTOWN  EDUCATION

Reading Math

Strategies for English Language Learners

High Beginning

 **Glencoe**

New York, New York   Columbus, Ohio   Chicago, Illinois   Peoria, Illinois   Woodland Hills, California

JAMESTOWN EDUCATION

Image Credits: Cover (cube)CORBIS, (calculator)Digital Vision, (globe)Creatas, (others)Getty Images.

The *McGraw·Hill* Companies

Send all inquiries to:
Glencoe/McGraw-Hill
8787 Orion Place
Columbus, OH 43240-4027

ISBN-13: 978-0-07-874227-9 (Student Edition)
ISBN-10: 0-07-874227-7 (Student Edition)
ISBN-13: 978-0-07-874230-9 (Teacher Edition)
ISBN-10: 0-07-874230-7 (Teacher Edition)

Printed in the United States of America.

1 2 3 4 5 6 7 8 9 10 066 11 10 09 08 07 06

Pronunciation Key

a	as in *an* or *cat*		**g**	as in *give, again,* or *dog*
ä	as in *father* or *arm*		**h**	as in *hat, whole,* or *ahead*
ā	as in *made, say,* or *maid*		**j**	as in *jar, enjoy, gentle,* or *badge*
e	as in *wet* or *sell*		**k**	as in *kitchen, book, mock,* or *cool*
ē	as in *he, see, mean, niece,* or *lovely*		**l**	as in *look, alive, heel, tall,* or *follow*
i	as in *in* or *fit*		**m**	as in *me, imagine,* or *seem*
ī	as in *I, mine, sigh, die,* or *my*		**n**	as in *no, inside, inning,* or *fun*
o	as in *on* or *not*		**ng**	as in *singer, bring,* or *drink*
ō	as in *fold, boat, own,* or *foe*		**p**	as in *put, open,* or *drop*
ô	as in *or, oar, naughty, awe,* or *ball*		**r**	as in *run, form,* or *wear*
oo	as in *good, would,* or *put*		**s**	as in *socks, herself,* or *miss*
o͞o	as in *roof* or *blue*		**sh**	as in *should, washing,* or *hash*
oi	as in *noise* or *joy*		**t**	as in *too, enter, mitten,* or *sit*
ou	as in *loud* or *now*		**th**	as in *think, nothing,* or *tooth*
u	as in *must* or *cover*		**t̲h̲**	as in *there, either,* or *smooth*
ū	as in *pure, cue, few,* or *feud*		**v**	as in *vote, even,* or *love*
ur	as in *turn, fern, heard, bird,* or *word*		**w**	as in *well* or *away*
ə	as in *awhile, model, second,* or *column*		**y**	as in *yellow* or *canyon*
b	as in *big, table,* or *job*		**z**	as in *zoo, hazy,* or *sizes*
ch	as in *chew, much,* or *latch*		**zh**	as in *seizure, measure,* or *mirage*
d	as in *deep, puddle,* or *mad*			
f	as in *fat, before, beef, stuff, graph,* or *rough*			

Before You Read

 Think about what you know. Read the lesson title above. What do you think the article will be about? Have you ever taken a long trip in a car? How many times did you have to stop to buy gas?

Vocabulary

The content-area and academic English words below appear in "Finding Your Car's Gas Mileage." Read the definitions and the example sentences.

Content-Area Words

mileage (mī′lij) the number of miles a car can travel on a certain amount of gas
Example: My small car gets good gas *mileage* on the highway.

gallon (gal′ən) a measurement of a certain amount of a liquid
Example: My family drinks one *gallon* of milk in two days.

odometer (ō dom′ə tər) a device in a car that measures how far the car has traveled
Example: The *odometer* showed how many miles I had driven to get to the beach.

instrument (in′strə mənt) a device that measures the condition or the work of something
Example: A thermometer is an *instrument* that measures a person's temperature.

speedometer (spē dom′ə tər) a device that measures how fast a car is traveling
Example: The *speedometer* shows that my car is traveling 45 miles per hour.

Academic English

affect (ə fekt′) to make something change
Example: Ice and snow may *affect* safety conditions on roads.

maintain (mān tān′) to keep something in good condition and able to work well
Example: I will *maintain* my bike by keeping it indoors when it rains.

Answer the questions below. Circle the part of each question that is the answer. The first one has been done for you.

1. Would a person find the *mileage* of a map or (of a truck)?
2. Does a *speedometer* show how fast a car is traveling or how far a car has traveled?
3. Would someone measure apples or water by the *gallon?*
4. If people *maintain* their cars, will the cars work well or break down?
5. Which *instrument* measures time, a thermometer or a clock?
6. Does pollution *affect* the air by making it dirty or by making it cold?
7. Does an *odometer* show the size of a car or the distance a car has traveled?

 Now skim the article and look for other words that are new to you. Write each new word and its definition in the Personal Dictionary.

While You Read

 Think about why you read. Different cars have different gas mileages. Do you know how to find the gas mileage of a car? As you read, look for the two pieces of information you need to find gas mileage.

Finding Your Car's Gas Mileage

₁ How often will your family need to stop for gas while driving on a trip? If you know the gas **mileage** of your car, you can find the answer. Gas mileage is the total number of miles your car travels on one **gallon** of gas. Your gas mileage is high when you can travel a long distance on one tank of gas.

₅ Many things **affect** the gas mileage of a car. Larger cars usually get lower gas mileage than smaller cars do. This is because larger cars are heavier and have larger engines. A large car filled with passengers gets even lower gas mileage. Small, fast sports cars have bigger engines than most small cars do. They often use more gas and have lower gas mileage than other small cars do.

₁₀ How and where you drive a car also affects gas mileage. When people drive in a city, they have to stop and start often. They may have to sit in traffic. This kind of driving can make a car use more gas. This makes its gas mileage go down. Gas mileage also goes down when a car travels up many tall hills. Cars usually get higher gas mileage when they travel on highways and at a steady, or regular, ₁₅ speed. Cars that people **maintain,** or service regularly, get better gas mileage too. Cars with tires that are inflated with enough air also get better mileage.

To find the gas mileage of a car, you must know two things. First, how many gallons does the gas tank hold? Second, how many miles can the car travel on one full tank of gas? The **odometer** in the car is the **instrument** that shows how many ₂₀ miles the car has traveled. It is usually on the dashboard near the **speedometer.** The speedometer is the instrument that tells you how fast the car is traveling.

For example, imagine that the odometer of your car shows 8,450 miles when you fill the tank with gas. By the time the tank becomes empty again, the odometer shows 8,930 miles. If you subtract 8,450 from 8,930, you find that your ₂₅ car has traveled 480 miles on one tank of gas. Now imagine that the gas tank in your car holds 20 gallons of gas. You now have everything you need to find the gas mileage. Divide the 480 miles you have traveled by the 20 gallons of gas. The gas mileage of your car is 24 miles per gallon.

What if the gas tank of your car holds 25 gallons instead of 20? The gas ₃₀ mileage would be lower. A trip of 480 miles divided by 25 gallons of gas would mean the car gets 19.2 miles per gallon.

LANGUAGE CONNECTION

Trip is a homograph, or a word that has more than one meaning. In the first sentence, *trip* means "a journey." Can you think of another meaning for the word *trip*?

CONTENT CONNECTION

Imagine that your car's gas tank holds 22 gallons, and that your car travels 440 miles on one tank. How can you use this information to find the gas mileage?

After You Read

A. Organizing Ideas

What things affect gas mileage? Complete the chart below. In the left column, list reasons why a car may get high gas mileage. In the right column, list reasons why a car may get low gas mileage. Use the article to find information. Some have been done for you.

High Gas Mileage	Low Gas Mileage
The car is small and light.	The car is large and heavy.
Few passengers are in the car.	
	The car travels on city streets where it starts and stops often.
The car travels on mostly flat surfaces.	
	The tires are not inflated with enough air.

Do you think school buses get good gas mileage? Write two or more sentences to answer this question. Did the chart help you answer this question? Why or why not?

_____

_____

_____

_____

B. Comprehension Skills

 Think about how to find answers. Look back at what you read. The information is in the text, but you may have to look in several sentences to find it.

Mark box **a, b,** or **c** with an **X** before the choice that best completes each sentence.

Recalling Facts

1. Gas mileage is the number of
   ☐ **a.** miles traveled on one tank of gas.
   ☐ **b.** gallons a gas tank holds.
   ☐ **c.** miles traveled on one gallon of gas.

2. To find gas mileage, a person must know
   ☐ **a.** the size of the gas tank.
   ☐ **b.** the price of one gallon of gas.
   ☐ **c.** the weight of the car.

3. The odometer measures
   ☐ **a.** the size of the gas tank.
   ☐ **b.** the number of miles traveled.
   ☐ **c.** how much gas is in the tank.

4. To find gas mileage, divide the number of miles traveled on a full tank by
   ☐ **a.** the cost of a full tank.
   ☐ **b.** the number of gallons in a full tank.
   ☐ **c.** the number of gallons left in the tank.

5. The gas mileage of a car driven in a city usually
   ☐ **a.** goes up.
   ☐ **b.** goes down.
   ☐ **c.** stays the same.

Understanding Ideas

1. From the article, you can conclude that driving on icy roads
   ☐ **a.** does not affect gas mileage.
   ☐ **b.** makes gas mileage go up.
   ☐ **c.** makes gas mileage go down.

2. A pickup truck probably has
   ☐ **a.** higher gas mileage than a small car.
   ☐ **b.** lower gas mileage than a small car.
   ☐ **c.** the same gas mileage as a small car.

3. If two cars have gas tanks of the same size, then
   ☐ **a.** the car with the larger engine goes farther on one tank.
   ☐ **b.** the car with the heavier load goes farther on one tank.
   ☐ **c.** the car that travels at a steady speed goes farther on one tank.

4. To maintain high gas mileage, a person could
   ☐ **a.** check the air in the car tires often.
   ☐ **b.** drive the same route every day.
   ☐ **c.** put heavy objects in the car.

5. People who regularly service their cars probably want to make sure that
   ☐ **a.** the gas tank is always full.
   ☐ **b.** the engine runs well.
   ☐ **c.** the car is clean.

C. Reading Strategies

1. Recognizing Words in Context

Find the word *inflated* in the article. One definition below is closest to the meaning of that word. One definition has the opposite or nearly the opposite meaning. The remaining definition has a meaning that has nothing to do with the word. Label the definitions **C** for *closest*, **O** for *opposite* or *nearly opposite*, and **U** for *unrelated*.

_____ **a.** full

_____ **b.** empty

_____ **c.** smooth

2. Distinguishing Fact from Opinion

Two of the statements below present *facts*, which can be proved. The other statement is an *opinion*, which expresses someone's thoughts or beliefs. Label the statements **F** for *fact* and **O** for *opinion*.

_____ **a.** Heavy cars usually get lower gas mileage than light cars.

_____ **b.** A car that is regularly serviced usually gets better gas mileage.

_____ **c.** A car with good gas mileage is more fun than a sports car.

3. Making Correct Inferences

Two of the statements below are correct *inferences,* or reasonable guesses, that are based on information in the article. The other statement is an incorrect inference. Label the statements **C** for *correct* inference and **I** for *incorrect* inference.

_____ **a.** A person whose car gets high gas mileage may spend less money on gas.

_____ **b.** Cars with large gas tanks get high gas mileage.

_____ **c.** A car may get better gas mileage on some trips than on others.

4. Understanding Main Ideas

One of the statements below expresses the main idea of the article. Another statement is too general, or too broad. The other explains only part of the article; it is too narrow. Label the statements **M** for *main idea*, **B** for *too broad*, and **N** for *too narrow*.

_____ **a.** The size of a car usually affects gas mileage.

_____ **b.** Many things affect the gas mileage of a car.

_____ **c.** Cars need gas in order to travel.

5. Responding to the Article

Complete the following sentence in your own words:

Before reading "Finding Your Car's Gas Mileage," I already knew

_____

_____

D. Expanding Vocabulary

Content-Area Words

Complete each sentence with a word from the box. Write the missing word on the line.

mileage	gallon	odometer	instrument	speedometer

1. The driver looked at the _____ to check his speed.

2. The mechanic used more than one _____ to service the car.

3. The price of a(n) _____ of gas changes often.

4. Her small car gets great gas _____ on flat, empty country roads.

5. The _____ in the new car has only 45 miles on it.

Academic English

In the article "Finding Your Car's Gas Mileage," you learned that *affect* means "to make something change." *Affect* can also mean "to cause feelings in," as in the following sentence.

This true story about a mother's love for her son will affect readers deeply.

Complete the sentence below.

1. When sad books *affect* me, I usually start to _____

Now use the word *affect* in a sentence of your own.

2. _____

_____

You also learned that *maintain* means "to keep something in good condition and able to work well." *Maintain* can also mean "to keep steady" or "to continue doing something," as in the following sentence.

I will maintain a speed of 55 miles per hour on the highway.

Complete the sentence below.

3. The tennis player wants to *maintain* her healthy diet so she can _____

Now use the word *maintain* in two sentences of your own.

4. _____

5. _____

 Share your new sentences with a partner.

Before You Read

 Think about what you know. Skim the article on the opposite page. Did you know that you can use different ways to measure temperature? What do you already know about how to measure temperature?

Vocabulary

The content-area and academic English words below appear in "Comparing Temperature Scales." Read the definitions and the example sentences.

Content-Area Words

temperature (tem′prə chər) a measurement of how hot or cold something is
   Example: The *temperature* outside is often low during winter.

thermometer (thər mom′ə tər) a device that measures temperature
   Example: The nurse put a *thermometer* in my mouth to check my body temperature.

scales (skālz) ways to measure things based on a certain series of steps
   Example: People may use different *scales* to measure temperature.

degrees (di grēz′) steps that add up to measure the amount of something
   Example: I wish the temperature in this warm room were a few *degrees* lower.

abbreviation (ə brē′vē ā′shən) one or more letters that represent a whole word or phrase
   Example: A common *abbreviation* for the word *junior* is "Jr."

Academic English

normal (nôr′məl) common or usual
   Example: Eggs and toast are *normal* breakfast foods at many restaurants.

range (rānj) the area between two limits, such as an upper limit and a lower limit
   Example: The age *range* of the students who attend our middle school is 11 to 14.

Read again the example sentences that follow the content-area and academic English word definitions. With a partner, discuss the meanings of the words and sentences.

 Now skim the article and look for other words that are new to you. Write each new word and its definition in the Personal Dictionary.

While You Read

 Think about why you read. What scale do you use to measure temperature? Would it be useful to know how to use other temperature scales? As you read, look for the names of three scales that people use to measure temperature.

Comparing
Temperature Scales

1 How warm is it outside today? You can find the answer to this question by checking the **temperature** on an outdoor **thermometer.** Several kinds of **scales** can measure temperature. One of these scales is the Fahrenheit (F) scale. It is named after Daniel Fahrenheit, the man who invented it. Another scale is the
5 Celsius (C), or centigrade, scale. *Centigrade* means "100 degrees." The Celsius scale is named after its inventor, Anders Celsius. Both scales use steps of equal size, or **degrees,** to measure temperature. However, the two scales use very different ways to find the degrees.

The **abbreviation** F or C with a degree symbol (°) shows a temperature. On
10 the Fahrenheit scale, the freezing point of water, or the temperature at which water freezes, is 32 degrees Fahrenheit (32°F). The boiling point of water, or the temperature at which water boils, is 212°F. The **normal** body temperature for humans is 98.6°F. People in the United States are the only people who use the Fahrenheit scale.

15 On the Celsius scale, the freezing point of water is zero degrees (0°C). The boiling point of water is 100°C. Normal human body temperature is 37°C. People first used the Celsius scale in Sweden and France almost 250 years ago. It is the scale that most people use today.

Lord Kelvin developed the Kelvin (K) temperature scale in the mid-1800s.
20 The zero point of this scale is equal to –273.15°C (–459.67°F). This zero point is the lowest possible temperature of anything in the world. Therefore some people call the Kelvin scale the "absolute temperature scale." On the Kelvin scale, the freezing point of water is 273.15K. The boiling point of water is 373.15K. Although scientists commonly use the Kelvin scale, most people rarely use it in
25 daily life.

Imagine that it is a summer day and you see a sign that shows the temperature as 25°C. How do you find the Fahrenheit temperature? Remember that the Celsius scale uses 100 degrees to show the **range** of temperatures between the freezing and boiling points of water. The Fahrenheit scale uses 180 degrees (32
30 through 212). This means that one Celsius degree is equal to 1.8 (180 ÷ 100) Fahrenheit degrees. First multiply the Celsius temperature by 1.8. Then add 32 degrees, because the freezing point in Fahrenheit is 32 degrees higher than it is in Celsius. If the temperature is 25°C, the first step is 25 × 1.8 = 45. The next step is 45 + 32 = 77. You have learned that 25°C is equal to 77°F.

LANGUAGE CONNECTION

Something that is "named after" a person has the same—or part of the same—name as that person. If you could name something after yourself, what would it be? What would you call it?

CONTENT CONNECTION

Just as people use different scales to measure temperature, they also use different systems to measure distance. The English system uses inches and feet. Another uses centimeters and meters. Do you know the name of the second system?

After You Read

A. Organizing Ideas

How can we compare the Fahrenheit scale and the Celsius scale? Complete the
diagram below. In the outer part of the left circle, list facts about the Fahrenheit scale.
In the outer part of the right circle, list facts about the Celsius scale. Where the circles
overlap, list things that the two scales have in common. Use the article to help you.
Some have been done for you.

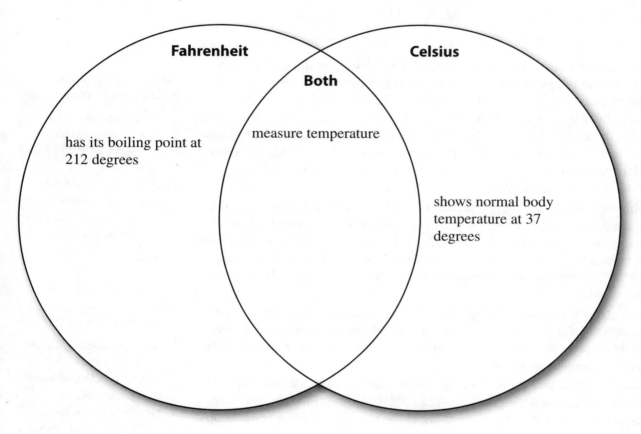

Fahrenheit

Both

Celsius

has its boiling point at
212 degrees

measure temperature

shows normal body
temperature at 37
degrees

Did the diagram help you compare the Fahrenheit and Celsius scales? Write two or
more sentences to describe how the scales are alike and different. What other things
could you compare by using this type of diagram?

_____

_____

_____

_____

B. Comprehension Skills

Tip! **Think about how to find answers.** Read each sentence below. Underline the words that will help you figure out how to complete each item.

Mark box **a, b,** or **c** with an **X** before the choice that best completes each sentence.

Recalling Facts

1. Another name for the Celsius scale is the
    ☐ **a.** U.S. scale.
    ☐ **b.** centigrade scale.
    ☐ **c.** Fahrenheit scale.

2. On the Celsius scale, water freezes at
    ☐ **a.** 0°C.
    ☐ **b.** 32°C.
    ☐ **c.** 37°C.

3. On the Celsius scale, water boils at
    ☐ **a.** 0°C.
    ☐ **b.** 32°C.
    ☐ **c.** 100°C.

4. On the Fahrenheit scale, water freezes at
    ☐ **a.** 0°F.
    ☐ **b.** 10°F.
    ☐ **c.** 32°F.

5. On the Fahrenheit scale, water boils at
    ☐ **a.** 100°F.
    ☐ **b.** 112°F.
    ☐ **c.** 212°F.

Understanding Ideas

1. From the article, you can conclude that
    ☐ **a.** the Kelvin scale is useful to scientists.
    ☐ **b.** the Celsius scale is not useful to scientists.
    ☐ **c.** the Fahrenheit scale is the scale that scientists use most often.

2. A temperature of 20°C is
    ☐ **a.** colder than 20°F.
    ☐ **b.** warmer than 20°F.
    ☐ **c.** the same as 20°F.

3. Multiply a temperature in degrees Celsius by 1.8 and add 32 to find the
    ☐ **a.** degrees Kelvin.
    ☐ **b.** degrees Celsius.
    ☐ **c.** degrees Fahrenheit.

4. The zero point of the Kelvin scale is
    ☐ **a.** hotter than the freezing point of water.
    ☐ **b.** colder than the freezing point of water.
    ☐ **c.** the same as 0°C.

5. Scientists commonly use the Kelvin scale because
    ☐ **a.** it is named after Lord Kelvin.
    ☐ **b.** they like to be different from other people.
    ☐ **c.** its zero point is the lowest temperature in the world.

C. Reading Strategies

1. Recognizing Words in Context

Find the word *commonly* in the article. One definition below is closest to the meaning of that word. One definition has the opposite or nearly the opposite meaning. The remaining definition has a meaning that has nothing to do with the word. Label the definitions **C** for *closest*, **O** for *opposite* or *nearly opposite*, and **U** for *unrelated*.

_____ **a.** rarely

_____ **b.** happily

_____ **c.** usually

2. Distinguishing Fact from Opinion

Two of the statements below present *facts*, which can be proved. The other statement is an *opinion*, which expresses someone's thoughts or beliefs. Label the statements **F** for *fact* and **O** for *opinion*.

_____ **a.** The Fahrenheit scale is the easiest temperature scale to use.

_____ **b.** One Celsius degree equals 1.8 Fahrenheit degrees.

_____ **c.** People in many countries use the Celsius scale.

3. Making Correct Inferences

Two of the statements below are correct *inferences*, or reasonable guesses, that are based on information in the article. The other statement is an incorrect inference. Label the statements **C** for *correct* inference and **I** for *incorrect* inference.

_____ **a.** Most people use the Celsius scale.

_____ **b.** Only the Celsius scale correctly measures body temperature.

_____ **c.** Most people do not need to use the Kelvin scale.

4. Understanding Main Ideas

One of the statements below expresses the main idea of the article. Another statement is too general, or too broad. The other explains only part of the article; it is too narrow. Label the statements **M** for *main idea*, **B** for *too broad*, and **N** for *too narrow*.

_____ **a.** People use three different scales to measure temperature.

_____ **b.** Most people use the Celsius scale today.

_____ **c.** A person can measure temperature in different ways.

5. Responding to the Article

Complete the following sentence in your own words:

From reading "Comparing Temperature Scales," I have learned

_____

_____

D. Expanding Vocabulary

Content-Area Words

Complete each analogy with a word from the box. Write in the missing word.

| temperature | thermometer | scales | degrees | abbreviation |

1. heavy : weight :: hot : _____

2. meal : snack :: word : _____

3. broken bone : X-ray :: fever : _____

4. build : tools :: measure : _____

5. height : inches :: heat : _____

Academic English

In the article "Comparing Temperature Scales," you learned that *normal* is an adjective that means "common or usual." *Normal* can also be a noun that means "the usual amount or level of something," as in the following sentence.

A sick person may have a temperature that is above normal.

Complete the sentence below.

1. Yesterday I got less sleep than *normal*, so I feel _____

Now use the word *normal* in a sentence of your own.

2. _____

_____

You also learned that *range* is a noun that means "the area between two limits, such as an upper limit and a lower limit." *Range* can also be a verb that means "to go from one limit to another," as in the following sentence.

The test grades range from very low to very high.

Complete the sentence below.

3. The grade levels at our school *range* from _____

Now use the word *range* in two sentences of your own.

4. _____

5. _____

Talk It Over Share your new sentences with a partner.

Before You Read

 Think about what you know. Read the title and the first paragraph of the article on the opposite page. Where have you seen percentages before?

Vocabulary

The content-area and academic English words below appear in "Percentages in Everyday Life." Read the definitions and the example sentences.

Content-Area Words

percentage (pər sen'tij) a part of a whole as it relates to 100
Example: A large *percentage* of students carry backpacks.

fraction (frak'shən) a part of a whole shown as a numerator over a denominator
Example: The *fraction* ½ represents one half.

denominator (di nom'ə nā´tər) the number below the line in a fraction by which the upper number is divided
Example: The number 2 is the *denominator* in the fraction ½.

symbol (sim'bəl) a letter or shape that represents something
Example: The *symbol* = means "equals."

comparison (kəm par'ə sən) an examination of how things are alike and different
Example: To choose my favorite food, I did a *comparison* of pizza and noodles.

Academic English

involve (in volv') to include as an important part
Example: My English classes always *involve* a lot of reading.

formula (fôr'myə lə) a way to find an answer
Example: In math class, the students learned a *formula* to find percentages.

Answer the questions below about the content-area and academic English words. Write your answers in the spaces provided. The first one has been done for you.

1. What word goes with *how to choose the most comfortable chair?* __comparison__

2. What word goes with *+ means "plus"?* _____

3. What word goes with *steps to solve a math problem?* _____

4. What word goes with *the bottom of a fraction?* _____

5. What word goes with *a part of 100?* _____

6. What word goes with *to include someone in an activity?* _____

7. What word goes with *⅗ or ¼?* _____

 Now skim the article and look for other words that are new to you. Write each new word and its definition in the Personal Dictionary.

While You Read

 Think about why you read. People use percentages in many daily activities. When have you used percentages? As you read, look for ways that percentages are helpful.

Percentages in Everyday Life

1   A **percentage** is a part of a whole. A percentage is a **fraction** with the **denominator** 100. But instead of using a fraction, such as $^{90}/_{100}$, people use the **symbol** %, as in 90%. In fact, the word *percent* means "of 100." If a student gets 90 answers correct on an exam that has 100 questions, his or her score is
5   90 percent (90%).

   Imagine that you need to wash 40 windows. After a while, you see that you have washed 8 of them. What percentage of the windows have you washed? To figure percentage, begin with the numbers you know and make a **comparison** to 100. In this example, you would figure that 8 windows is to 40 windows as X% is
10 to 100%. To find the number X, continue to work with the numbers you know. First multiply 8 by 100, which equals 800. Then divide 800 by the other known number (40). You learn that you have washed 20% of the windows.

   Many of the things people buy **involve** percentages. For example, the label on a shirt may say *65% cotton, 35% silk*. Different foods provide different percentages
15 of things people should eat each day, such as proteins, vitamins, and other nutrients. Many soda and water bottles are made from a percentage of recycled plastic. Also, many paper products contain a percentage of recycled paper.

   Imagine that you and your friends decide to go to the mall. You have the money you earned when you washed the windows. You find a winter coat that
20 you want to buy. The sign shows that it is 30% off the regular price. The regular price is $90. You need to know how much money you will save if you buy this coat. Begin with the known numbers. You know you will save 30%. Think of the **formula,** or way of calculating, as 30% is to 100% as $X is to $90. First multiply the known numbers, 30 × 90, which equals 2,700. Then divide this
25 number by 100. The answer is 27. You will save $27. When you subtract this amount from $90, the sale price is $63.

   The store charges a sales tax on purchases, or things that people buy. This tax is a percentage too. If the tax is 6% on your $63 purchase, your tax is $3.78 (6 × $63 = $378, and $378 ÷ 100 = $3.78).
30 Later you and your friends go to a restaurant. The bill is $14.40. Your friends ask you to calculate the 15% tip. No problem, right?

LANGUAGE CONNECTION

The word *percentage* is made of the root word *percent* and the suffix *-age*. What is the root word in *mileage*?

CONTENT CONNECTION

To find the price of an item that is 30% off, first find 30% of the item's regular price. Then subtract that amount from the regular price. Would you rather buy a $100 coat when it is 25% off or 40% off?

After You Read

A. Applying the Math

Can you use what you know about percentages? Complete the flowchart below. Use what you have learned about percentages to find the total cost of an item that is on sale. Fill in the numbers that you need to use in each step.

Problem

I want to buy a backpack that I see in a store. The tag says that the backpack is $20. A sign shows that all backpacks are 25% off. Sales tax is 5%. What will the backpack cost?

Task 1: Find the sale price.

Step 1: Multiply 20 by 25, which equals 500.

Step 2: Divide 500 by _____, which equals 5.
This is the amount to subtract from the regular price.

Step 3: Subtract _____ from the original price of the backpack: _____.

The sale price is _____.

Task 2: Find the sales tax.

Step 1: Multiply the sale price of _____ by the sales tax percentage of _____, which equals 75.

Step 2: Divide _____ by _____, which equals _____. This is the sales tax.

Task 3: Find the total cost.

Add the sales tax, or _____ cents, to the _____ that the backpack costs.

This equals _____.

Solution

The total cost of the backpack is _____.

Did this flowchart help you understand how to find the total cost of an item that is on sale? Write two or more sentences about the steps a person takes to find the total cost.

_____

_____

B. Comprehension Skills

 Think about how to find answers. Think about what each sentence means. Try to say it to yourself in your own words before you complete it.

Mark box **a, b,** or **c** with an **X** before the choice that best completes each sentence.

Recalling Facts

1. A percentage is
- ☐ **a.** a part of a whole.
- ☐ **b.** a number higher than 100.
- ☐ **c.** a number that is stated in tenths.

2. The word *percent* means
- ☐ **a.** "of part."
- ☐ **b.** "of 100."
- ☐ **c.** "of a cent."

3. An item that is on sale at 30% off costs
- ☐ **a.** 30% less than the regular price.
- ☐ **b.** 40% less than the regular price.
- ☐ **c.** 70% less than the regular price.

4. The sales tax of an item that is on sale is
- ☐ **a.** included in the sale price.
- ☐ **b.** a percentage of the sale price.
- ☐ **c.** a percentage of the regular price.

5. To find a percentage, begin with the known numbers and
- ☐ **a.** divide by 100.
- ☐ **b.** multiply by 100.
- ☐ **c.** make a comparison to 100.

Understanding Ideas

1. If a pair of shoes is 20% off and the sale price is $80, the regular price is
- ☐ **a.** $60.
- ☐ **b.** $100.
- ☐ **c.** $120.

2. A student who scores 70% on a test has more correct answers than a student who scores
- ☐ **a.** 65%.
- ☐ **b.** 75%.
- ☐ **c.** 85%.

3. To figure the percentage of cookies sold at a bake sale, first find out
- ☐ **a.** how many cookies were sold.
- ☐ **b.** how many cookies were baked.
- ☐ **c.** both the number of cookies baked and the number of cookies sold.

4. If someone correctly answers 40 out of 50 test questions, his or her score is
- ☐ **a.** 40%.
- ☐ **b.** 80%.
- ☐ **c.** 90%.

5. If a sign says *Buy two for the price of one,* it means that someone who buys two items saves
- ☐ **a.** 50 cents.
- ☐ **b.** 100%.
- ☐ **c.** 50%.

C. Reading Strategies

1. Recognizing Words in Context

Find the word *figure* in the article. One definition below is closest to the meaning of that word. One definition has the opposite or nearly the opposite meaning. The remaining definition has a meaning that has nothing to do with the word. Label the definitions **C** for *closest*, **O** for *opposite* or *nearly opposite*, and **U** for *unrelated*.

_____ **a.** wonder about

_____ **b.** find out

_____ **c.** talk about

2. Distinguishing Fact from Opinion

Two of the statements below present *facts*, which can be proved. The other statement is an *opinion*, which expresses someone's thoughts or beliefs. Label the statements **F** for *fact* and **O** for *opinion*.

_____ **a.** Sales tax is a percentage of the purchase price.

_____ **b.** Fractions are easier to understand than percentages.

_____ **c.** To find percentage, make a comparison to 100.

3. Making Correct Inferences

Two of the statements below are correct *inferences*, or reasonable guesses, that are based on information in the article. The other statement is an incorrect inference. Label the statements **C** for *correct* inference and **I** for *incorrect* inference.

_____ **a.** A product on sale is sold at a fair price.

_____ **b.** Some recycled material can be used to make new products.

_____ **c.** Many people use percentages when they leave tips at restaurants.

4. Understanding Main Ideas

One of the statements below expresses the main idea of the article. Another statement is too general, or too broad. The other explains only part of the article; it is too narrow. Label the statements **M** for *main idea*, **B** for *too broad*, and **N** for *too narrow*.

_____ **a.** Percentages can be helpful to a person.

_____ **b.** People can use percentages to find sale prices.

_____ **c.** People can find percentages by making comparisons to 100.

5. Responding to the Article

Complete the following sentences in your own words:

One of the things I did best while reading "Percentages in Everyday Life" was

_____

I think that I did this well because _____

_____

D. Expanding Vocabulary

Content-Area Words

Read each item carefully. Write on the line the word or phrase that best completes each sentence.

1. The denominator is the part of a fraction that is _____.

    above the line   below the line   behind the line

2. A percentage compares an amount to _____.

    a sale price   100   a fraction

3. In a fraction, the numerator is divided by _____.

    the denominator   the number 100   the percent

4. The symbol $ means _____.

    "and"   "percentage"   "dollars"

5. When shoppers do a comparison, they look at _____.

    differences between things   only one thing   the colors of things

Academic English

In the article "Percentages in Everyday Life," you learned that *involve* means "to include as an important part." *Involve* can also mean "to take up the attention of someone completely," as in the following sentence.

    This game is so interesting that it will involve you for hours.

Complete the sentence below.

1. A toy may *involve* a child for _____

Now use the word *involve* in a sentence of your own.

2. _____

You also learned that *formula* means "a way to find an answer." *Formula* can also mean "a set of steps or items that will create a result," as in the following sentence.

    The painter used a formula to mix colors to create a certain shade of blue.

Complete the sentence below.

3. Healthy foods and exercise are part of a *formula* to _____

Now use the word *formula* in two sentences of your own.

4. _____

5. _____

 Share your new sentences with a partner.

Before You Read

 Think about what you know. Read the lesson title above. What do you think the article will be about? When was the last time you used a map? What kind of map did you use?

Vocabulary

The content-area and academic English words below appear in "Using a Road Map." Read the definitions and the example sentences.

Content-Area Words

representation (rep´ri zen tā´shən) something that looks like or stands for something else
　　Example: The Statue of Liberty is a *representation* of a woman holding a torch.

scale (skāl) the relationship between sizes on a map and sizes on Earth's surface
　　Example: The map *scale* shows that 1 inch on the map equals 10 miles.

relationship (ri lā´shən ship´) a connection or link between things
　　Example: Doctors understand the *relationship* between exercise and good health.

ratio (rā´shē ō´) the relationship between the amount, number, or size of two things
　　Example: Our class *ratio* is two boys to every girl.

detail (dē´tāl) the small features or parts of something
　　Example: A person must stand close to that painting to see the *detail*.

Academic English

area (ār´ē ə) a particular surface, space, or region
　　Example: A desert is a dry *area*.

locate (lō´kāt) to find the exact place or position of something
　　Example: It was hard to *locate* my brother on the crowded playground.

Rate each vocabulary word according to the following scale. Write a number next to each content-area and academic English word.

<u>4</u>　I have never seen the word before.

<u>3</u>　I have seen the word but do not know what it means.

<u>2</u>　I know what the word means when I read it.

<u>1</u>　I use the word myself in speaking or writing.

 Now skim the article and look for other words that are new to you. Write each new word and its definition in the Personal Dictionary.

While You Read

Tip! **Think about why you read.** Do you know how to figure out how long it will take you to get somewhere? As you read, look for the two pieces of information you need to figure out travel time.

Using a Road Map

1   **M**aps provide interesting and useful pictures of all kinds of places. Usually a map is a **representation** of a part of Earth's surface. The people who make maps are called *mapmakers*. Mapmakers include a map **scale** on each map that they make. The map scale shows the **relationship** between the distances on the

5 map and actual distances on Earth. Map scales show this relationship as a **ratio.** A map of a town may have a ratio of 1:100,000. This ratio means that 1 inch on the map equals 100,000 inches on Earth. To find the number of miles in 100,000 inches, a person must first know that 1 mile is equal to 63,360 inches. Then the person can calculate that $100,000 \div 63,360 = 1.58$. In this example, 1 inch on

10 the map is equal to 1.58 miles on Earth.

   Some maps are small-scale maps, and others are large-scale maps. A small-scale map shows a large **area** with a small amount of **detail.** A large-scale map shows a small area with a large amount of detail. One way to understand this idea is to imagine that you are floating in a balloon above your town. The ratio of the

15 area you see below you may be 1:10,000. As the balloon rises, the details become smaller. The scale also becomes smaller. An example of a small-scale map is a map with the ratio 1:1,000,000.

   Road maps, like many other maps, show the distance in miles between places. Road maps are large-scale maps. However, road maps usually do not show the

20 large ratio of one inch to thousands or hundreds of thousands of inches. They often show only the smaller ratio of one inch to a certain number of miles.

   Imagine that you must use a map scale on a road map to find the distance from your town to the state capital. When you **locate** your town and the capital on the map, you see that one direct road connects them. The scale shows that 1 inch is

25 equal to 25 miles. You measure the distance on the map between your town and the capital. They are 7 inches apart. That means the state capital is 175 (7×25) miles from your town.

   Now imagine that a town called Centerville is between your town and the capital. It is 3 inches from your town, or 75 miles away. You have to buy a new

30 soccer shirt there. You want to calculate the amount of time it takes to travel to Centerville. First you need to know your travel speed, or how fast you plan to travel. You must also know the number of miles you need to travel. The speed limit is 55 miles per hour. If you travel at that speed, you will get to Centerville in about 82 minutes (75 miles $\div$ 55 miles per hour $= 1.36$ hours;

35 1.36 hours $\times$ 60 minutes per hour $= 82$ minutes).

CONTENT CONNECTION

Imagine that you have two maps of the same size. One map uses a ratio of 1 inch to 2 miles. The other uses a ratio of 1 inch to 10 miles. Which map shows a larger area?

LANGUAGE CONNECTION

Sometimes a noun acts as an adjective. Although the word *road* is a noun, it acts as an adjective in the phrase *road maps. Road* describes a kind of map. In the phrase *world map,* does *world* act as a noun or as an adjective?

After You Read

A. Applying the Math

Can you draw a map to scale? Draw a map of places to go in Sunnytown. Use the map scale to measure the distances between the different places. You can draw each place in any direction.

Map of Sunnytown, U.S.A.

Scale: One inch equals 1 mile. The following line is equal to 1 inch: ├─────┼─────┤

Make a measuring tool. Cut a piece of paper that is as long as the scale line. Use the tool to make your map.

Places to Go in Sunnytown:

Sunny Park – Sunny Park is in the center of town.

Clear Lake – The lake is .5 mile from Sunny Park.

Art Museum – The museum is 1.5 miles from Clear Lake.

Sunnytown School – The school is 1 mile from Sunny Park.

Town Library – The library is 2 miles from Sunnytown School.

Green Farm – The farm is 1 mile from Clear Lake.

•

Sunny Park

Did making the map help you understand how to use a map scale? Write two or more sentences to explain what you learned about maps and map scales. What is another way you could use the type of measuring tool you used to make your map? Explain your answer.

B. Comprehension Skills

 Think about how to find answers. Look back at different parts of the text. What facts help you figure out how to complete the sentences?

Mark box **a, b,** or **c** with an **X** before the choice that best completes each sentence.

Recalling Facts

1. A map scale
   - ☐ **a.** is a representation of Earth's surface.
   - ☐ **b.** shows the distance in miles between places.
   - ☐ **c.** shows the relationship between distances on the map and real distances on Earth.

2. A small-scale map shows
   - ☐ **a.** how big Earth is.
   - ☐ **b.** a large area with a small amount of detail.
   - ☐ **c.** a small area with a large amount of detail.

3. A map ratio of 1:750,000 means that
   - ☐ **a.** 1 inch equals 750 miles.
   - ☐ **b.** 1 inch equals 750,000 miles.
   - ☐ **c.** 1 inch equals 750,000 inches.

4. The number of inches in a mile is
   - ☐ **a.** 1.58.
   - ☐ **b.** 63,360.
   - ☐ **c.** 100,000.

5. To calculate travel time, a person needs to know both the number of miles he or she has to travel and
   - ☐ **a.** the speed limit.
   - ☐ **b.** the travel speed.
   - ☐ **c.** what time the trip starts.

Understanding Ideas

1. A ratio is
   - ☐ **a.** a type of relationship between two things.
   - ☐ **b.** a number that expresses amount.
   - ☐ **c.** the difference between scales.

2. A map with the scale ratio 1:10,000,000 is an example of a
   - ☐ **a.** large-scale map.
   - ☐ **b.** small-scale map.
   - ☐ **c.** medium-scale map.

3. A scale ratio of 1:10,000 represents more miles per inch than a ratio of
   - ☐ **a.** 1:1,100.
   - ☐ **b.** 1:10,100.
   - ☐ **c.** 1:100,000.

4. From the article, you can conclude that a person would use a small-scale map to
   - ☐ **a.** find the nearest park.
   - ☐ **b.** locate an island in the Pacific Ocean.
   - ☐ **c.** find a place that is 15 miles away.

5. You can also conclude that, if 1 inch on your map equals 20 miles, and you must visit a city that is 6 map inches from your town,
   - ☐ **a.** you must travel 20 miles.
   - ☐ **b.** you must travel 60 miles.
   - ☐ **c.** you must travel 120 miles.

C. Reading Strategies

1. Recognizing Words in Context

Find the word *direct* in the article. One definition below is closest to the meaning of that word. One definition has the opposite or nearly the opposite meaning. The remaining definition has a meaning that has nothing to do with the word. Label the definitions **C** for *closest*, **O** for *opposite* or *nearly opposite*, and **U** for *unrelated*.

_____ **a.** clean

_____ **b.** straight

_____ **c.** curved

2. Distinguishing Fact from Opinion

Two of the statements below present *facts*, which can be proved. The other statement is an *opinion*, which expresses someone's thoughts or beliefs. Label the statements **F** for *fact* and **O** for *opinion*.

_____ **a.** A small-scale map is not as useful as a large-scale map.

_____ **b.** A map scale helps a person figure out the distance between places.

_____ **c.** A small-scale map shows a small amount of detail.

3. Making Correct Inferences

Two of the statements below are correct *inferences*, or reasonable guesses, that are based on information in the article. The other statement is an incorrect inference. Label the statements **C** for *correct* inference and **I** for *incorrect* inference.

_____ **a.** Large-scale maps help people find roads to travel short distances.

_____ **b.** Map scales tell people how long it will take to travel between places.

_____ **c.** A map that shows many countries is probably a small-scale map.

4. Understanding Main Ideas

One of the statements below expresses the main idea of the article. Another statement is too general, or too broad. The other explains only part of the article; it is too narrow. Label the statements **M** for *main idea*, **B** for *too broad*, and **N** for *too narrow*.

_____ **a.** Maps are useful for travel because they show roads.

_____ **b.** Maps include scales that help people figure out distances.

_____ **c.** Small-scale maps and large-scale maps show different amounts of detail.

5. Responding to the Article

Complete the following sentence in your own words:

One thing in "Using a Road Map" that I cannot understand is

_____

_____

D. Expanding Vocabulary

Content-Area Words

Cross out one word in each row that is not related to the word in dark type.

1. representation	likeness	house	painting	picture
2. scale	map	ratio	book	distance
3. relationship	first	connection	link	between
4. ratio	comparison	two	sound	size
5. detail	small	close	features	snake

Academic English

In the article "Using a Road Map," you learned that *area* means "a particular surface, space, or region." *Area* can also mean "a type of interest or job," as in the following sentence.

Math is my favorite area of study.

Complete the sentence below.

1. Some people who work in the *area* of medicine are _____

Now use the word *area* in a sentence of your own.

2. _____

_____

You also learned that *locate* means "to find the exact place or position of something." *Locate* can also mean "to settle oneself in a particular place to live," as in the following sentence.

He plans to locate himself in Chicago after he graduates from school.

Complete the sentence below.

3. The place where I would most like to *locate* myself is _____

Now use the word *locate* in two sentences of your own.

4. _____

5. _____

 Share your new sentences with a partner.

Before You Read

Tip! **Think about what you know.** Read the lesson title above. What is your favorite thing to buy from the grocery store? What is the highest price you would pay for it?

Vocabulary

The content-area and academic English words below appear in "Shopping for the Best Value." Read the definitions and the example sentences.

Content-Area Words

value (val′ū) a good price for the quality and amount of an item or service
> *Example:* I shop at stores where I get the best *value* for my money.

product (prod′əkt) something that people can buy
> *Example:* Cereal is my favorite breakfast *product*.

compare (kəm pār′) to examine how things are alike and different
> *Example:* The girls stood next to each other to *compare* their heights.

quantity (kwon′tə tē) the amount or number of something
> *Example:* He felt sick after he ate a large *quantity* of candy.

units (ū′nits) specific amounts that people use to measure the quantity of something
> *Example:* Miles are common *units* of distance.

Academic English

item (ī′təm) something that is part of a larger group or set
> *Example:* Bread is one *item* that my mom buys at the grocery store.

purchase (pur′chəs) to buy something
> *Example:* I have enough money to *purchase* one CD.

Do any of the words above seem related? Sort the seven vocabulary words into three categories. Write the words down on note cards or in a chart. Words may fit into more than one group. You may wish to work with a partner for this activity. Label the categories *Things People Shop For, Ways People Measure When They Shop,* and *Other*.

 Now skim the article and look for other words that are new to you. Write each new word and its definition in the Personal Dictionary.

While You Read

Tip! **Think about why you read.** What is the most recent item that you have bought? Did you choose it because of the price or the brand, or did you choose it for another reason? As you read, think about the things that help people decide what to buy.

Shopping for the Best Value

1   Careful grocery shoppers may have difficulty if they try to make a "quick trip" to the market. They often need time to find the best **value** for their money. They wonder if they should buy the large can or the small can of vegetables. They think about whether one **product** tastes better than another. People who look for
5 the best value **compare** products to look at how an **item** is similar to and different from others.

  A person who compares prices should be sure that the **quantity,** or amount, of each item is the same. If the quantity is different, the shopper may not choose the best value. Shoppers can buy items such as milk and orange juice in different
10 **units** of measure. Gallons, quarts, pints, and ounces are four of the most common units of measure. Each gallon holds four quarts. Each quart holds two pints. Each pint holds 16 ounces. A shopper who compares items of different quantities must think about the price per unit of measure.

  People usually buy milk in gallons, half gallons, or quarts. Imagine that a
15 gallon of White Star milk costs $2.99. A half gallon costs $1.79. A quart costs $1.19. Which is the best value? At first it may seem that the quart and half gallon are better values because they are cheaper than the gallon. To compare prices, however, remember to compare the same amount of each product. Two quarts of milk, which equal one half gallon, cost $2.38 ($1.19 $\times$ 2). That means the half
20 gallon that costs $1.79 is a better value than the two quarts. Two half gallons of milk, which equal one full gallon, cost $3.58 ($1.79 $\times$ 2). The gallon of milk that costs $2.99 is cheaper by $0.59. Usually larger quantities are cheaper per unit than smaller quantities.

  You may think that it is always best to **purchase** the largest quantity of an
25 item. However, if your family does not drink a gallon of milk in a week, the milk may spoil. In this case, the smaller quantity at a higher price per unit may be the better choice. You may feel that Blue Circle milk tastes better than White Star milk. Although a gallon of Blue Circle milk costs $3.69, you choose Blue Circle because it is a better value for you. It is not always best to purchase the largest
30 quantity or the cheapest brand of a product. When you think about all of your choices, you can make the best decision about the value of a product.

CONTENT CONNECTION

Common units of measure for liquids are gallons, quarts, pints, and ounces. Can you think of any common units of measure for distances? Hint: What units would you use to measure your height?

LANGUAGE CONNECTION

The endings -er and -est, when added to an adjective such as large, form new adjectives that compare items. Think of a school, Earth, and a mountain. Which is large? Larger? Largest?

After You Read

A. Organizing Ideas

What is a good value for you? Complete the form below. First, read the example. Then, in the first column, list three items that you have bought recently. In the second, third, and fourth columns, draw a circle around *excellent, average,* or *poor* to rate the items you bought. In the last column, circle *yes* or *no* to tell whether you compared items before you made your choice.

Example:

Item	Quality	Price	Quantity	Did I compare items?
socks	excellent average (poor)	excellent (average) poor	(excellent) average poor	yes (no)

Your List:

Item	Quality	Price	Quantity	Did I compare items?
	excellent average poor	excellent average poor	excellent average poor	yes no
	excellent average poor	excellent average poor	excellent average poor	yes no
	excellent average poor	excellent average poor	excellent average poor	yes no

What did you learn about the items you buy? Do you look for good values when you shop? Write two or more sentences to answer these questions. Would you use this type of form again? Why or why not?

_____

_____

_____

B. Comprehension Skills

 Think about how to find answers. Look back at what you read. The words in an answer are usually contained in a single sentence.

Mark box **a, b,** or **c** with an **X** before the choice that best completes each sentence.

Recalling Facts

1. To look for the best value, a shopper needs to
   ☐ **a.** compare items.
   ☐ **b.** find the cheapest brand.
   ☐ **c.** look for the largest quantity.

2. To compare items, a shopper should make sure that
   ☐ **a.** the product brands are the same.
   ☐ **b.** the prices of the items are the same.
   ☐ **c.** the quantities of the items are the same.

3. In the article, a half gallon compared to a gallon of White Star milk
   ☐ **a.** tastes better.
   ☐ **b.** has a cheaper price per unit.
   ☐ **c.** has a more expensive price per unit.

4. Large quantities and cheap brands are
   ☐ **a.** never the best choices.
   ☐ **b.** always the best choices.
   ☐ **c.** not always the best choices.

5. One gallon is the same quantity as
   ☐ **a.** six quarts.
   ☐ **b.** two quarts.
   ☐ **c.** four quarts.

Understanding Ideas

1. From the article, you can conclude that
   ☐ **a.** items that cost more taste better.
   ☐ **b.** a good value is not the same for all people.
   ☐ **c.** people who shop for value always pay less for groceries.

2. You can also conclude that finding a good value
   ☐ **a.** is a fun way to pass the time.
   ☐ **b.** is a waste of time.
   ☐ **c.** usually takes time.

3. Gallons, quarts, pints, and ounces are units of
   ☐ **a.** measurement.
   ☐ **b.** distance.
   ☐ **c.** price.

4. To find the best value, a shopper may want to compare
   ☐ **a.** two items rather than three items.
   ☐ **b.** three items rather than two items.
   ☐ **c.** large items rather than small items.

5. Four quarts of paint probably will
   ☐ **a.** cost less than a gallon of the same paint.
   ☐ **b.** cost more than a gallon of the same paint.
   ☐ **c.** be a better value than a gallon of the same paint.

C. Reading Strategies

1. Recognizing Words in Context

Find the word *spoil* in the article. One definition below is closest to the meaning of that word. One definition has the opposite or nearly the opposite meaning. The remaining definition has a meaning that has nothing to do with the word. Label the definitions **C** for *closest*, **O** for *opposite* or *nearly opposite*, and **U** for *unrelated*.

_____ **a.** become fresh

_____ **b.** turn white

_____ **c.** go bad

2. Distinguishing Fact from Opinion

Two of the statements below present *facts*, which can be proved. The other statement is an *opinion*, which expresses someone's thoughts or beliefs. Label the statements **F** for *fact* and **O** for *opinion*.

_____ **a.** A pint is equal to 16 ounces.

_____ **b.** Quantity is the most important part of a good value.

_____ **c.** The cheapest item is not always the best value.

3. Making Correct Inferences

Two of the statements below are correct *inferences*, or reasonable guesses, that are based on information in the article. The other statement is an incorrect inference. Label the statements **C** for *correct* inference and **I** for *incorrect* inference.

_____ **a.** Sometimes the most expensive item is the best value.

_____ **b.** People choose some items for cost and other items for different reasons.

_____ **c.** People should compare items only if they are worried about cost.

4. Understanding Main Ideas

One of the statements below expresses the main idea of the article. Another statement is too general, or too broad. The other explains only part of the article; it is too narrow. Label the statements **M** for *main idea*, **B** for *too broad*, and **N** for *too narrow*.

_____ **a.** Shoppers should compare items to get the best value for them.

_____ **b.** Different people choose to buy different products.

_____ **c.** Large quantities of a product are often cheaper than small quantities.

5. Responding to the Article

Complete the following sentence in your own words:

What interested me most in "Shopping for the Best Value" was

_____

_____

D. Expanding Vocabulary

Content-Area Words

Complete each sentence with a word from the box. Write the missing word on the line.

| value | product | compare | quantity | units |

1. A _____ is something that a person buys in a store.

2. Careful shoppers look for the best _____ for their money.

3. Shoppers look at the _____ of measurement when they compare items.

4. Hector should _____ the three skateboards before he buys one.

5. Big families often shop for items that stores sell in a large _____.

Academic English

In the article "Shopping for the Best Value," you learned that *item* means "something that is part of a larger group or set." *Item* can also mean "a piece of information, such as a short article in a newspaper," as in the following sentence.

I read an interesting newspaper item about the new restaurant.

Complete the sentence below.

1. I will write an *item* for our school newspaper about _____

Now use the word *item* in a sentence of your own.

2. _____

_____

You also learned that *purchase* is a verb that means "to buy something."
Purchase can also be a noun that means "something that someone buys,"
as in the following sentence.

An umbrella is a smart purchase if you live in a rainy climate.

Complete the sentence below.

3. The store clerk put my *purchase* into a _____

Now use the word *purchase* in two sentences of your own.

4. _____

5. _____

 Share your new sentences with a partner.

Writing a Journal Entry

Read the journal entry. Then complete the sentences. Use words from the Word Bank.

Word Bank

mileage   purchase

locate   involve

compare

June 15

Today my family begins a long road trip to visit my aunt and uncle. The

trip will (1)_____ many types of roads. We will drive on wide

highways through cities and on narrow roads through mountains. I want

to stay awake so that I can (2)_____ all the different sights.

Along the way, we will stop at museums and other interesting places. My

job is to (3)_____ these places on our map. My dad says we will

not have to (4)_____ gas often, because our car gets good gas

(5)_____ .

Reading an Advertisement

Read the advertisement. Circle the word that completes each sentence.

Clean Your Kitchen While You Sit on the Couch!

It can be hard to (**detail, maintain**) a clean kitchen. Surfaces, such as countertops, floors, and cabinets, collect germs and dirt. Working hard to keep these surfaces clean may (**affect, value**) the way you feel.

Don't Wait! Buy the Amazing Walking Washcloth Today!

You may feel tired, or you may not have enough energy to do other things. But a new (**product, abbreviation**) called the Walking Washcloth can scrub these surfaces clean while you enjoy your life. The Walking Washcloth is not a (**fraction, normal**) washcloth. It moves by itself across countertops and floors. It can also pull itself up walls and cabinet doors. It can clean almost every (**area, gallon**) of your kitchen.

 **Making Connections**

Work with a partner. Talk about what the words mean. How can you use the words to talk about a car? List your ideas in the outline of the car below.

temperature	range	formula	symbol	item
instrument	scales	odometer	units	ratio

Use all of the words above in complete sentences of your own. Each sentence may include one or more of the words. To help you start writing, look at the ideas you wrote about. After you write your sentences, read them over. If you find a mistake, correct it.

_____

_____

_____

_____

_____

_____

_____

_____

_____

Catering an Event

Before You Read

 Think about what you know. Read the title and the first paragraph of the article on the opposite page. Why do you think people need help when they decide to have parties or large meetings?

Vocabulary

The content-area and academic English words below appear in "Catering an Event." Read the definitions and the example sentences.

Content-Area Words

host (hōst) to have a party, meeting, or other event that guests attend
   Example: The school will *host* a science fair this year.

event (i vent') an important thing that occurs; a gathering of people for a purpose
   Example: Jamal's college graduation was an important *event*.

caterers (kā'tər ərz) people who provide food and other services for an event
   Example: People often hire *caterers* to prepare food for parties.

budget (buj'it) a plan to use a certain amount of money for a set purpose
   Example: I have a *budget* of $35 to buy CDs.

adjustments (ə just'mənts) changes that help to reach a goal
   Example: To get a better grade on her paper, Tina made some *adjustments* to the grammar.

Academic English

selection (si lek'shən) a group of things to choose from
   Example: The bakery had a big *selection* of cakes and pies.

final (fīn'əl) last; at the end of something
   Example: The letter *z* is the *final* letter in the alphabet.

Answer the questions below. Circle the part of each question that is the answer. The first one has been done for you.

1. Which *event* is on the date someone was born, a wedding or (a birthday)?
2. Does a person make a *budget* before an event or after an event?
3. Is lunch or dinner the *final* meal of the day?
4. Would *adjustments* to size and length or to color and price help clothes fit better?
5. Would someone *host* a business meeting or a family party at home?
6. Does a library offer a *selection* of food or of books?
7. Would *caterers* at an event serve food or dance with guests?

 Now skim the article and look for other words that are new to you. Write each new word and its definition in the Personal Dictionary.

While You Read

 Think about why you read. Have you ever been to a party where caterers served the guests? How do you think caterers decide how much to charge for their services? As you read, try to find the answer.

Catering an Event

1 Sometimes people want to **host** an **event,** such as a business meeting or a birthday party. These people may hire **caterers** to provide food and services. Caterers are people in businesses that prepare and serve food for events. Some caterers also provide music, gifts, and decorations.

5 Caterers need to ask several questions to learn what services people want for an event. How many guests will attend the event? What kind of food should the caterers prepare and serve? How much food will the guests need? Will the guests serve themselves with food from a buffet? Will servers bring food to the guests' tables? What kinds of drinks will the guests want?

10 People who hire caterers usually decide on a **budget,** or a plan to use a certain amount of money, for the entire event. To make a budget, people need to know how much money the caterer charges for the items they want. Then they must make **adjustments** so that the total cost fits within the budget.

For example, imagine that a company called Apex Hammers wants to host a 15 business meeting for 250 new workers. Apex hires Candy's Catering Company to serve lunch. Apex also wants Candy's to provide small key chain hammers as gifts for each of the guests. Apex sets the budget for the event at $5,000. This means that Apex wants to spend about $20 per person ($5,000 ÷ 250 = $20).

Candy's charges $20 per person to serve lunch at tables, so the food will cost 20 $5,000. Apex will not have money left for the gifts, which cost $300. Apex and Candy's then work together to make a few changes to the plans. Candy's tells Apex that the cost for a buffet lunch is only $12 per person. This is a total of $3,000 (250 × $12). The cost for a buffet is less because Candy's would not have to pay as many servers. Apex agrees to the change. Then Apex learns that 25 Candy's charges an additional $5 per person for a **selection** of desserts. This is a total of $1,250 (250 × $5). Apex decides to add the desserts to the menu. The **final** cost of the desserts, the buffet, and the gifts is $4,550. Apex still has $450 left in its budget.

Candy's has to think about its budget too. The caterers have to buy food as 30 well as special containers to carry it to events. Candy's also has to buy and take care of vans or other types of cars to deliver the food. Candy's must pay cooks and servers. Candy's figures out how much these things cost. The caterers add these costs to the amount they charge people for their services.

LANGUAGE CONNECTION

In the phrase *the guests' tables,* the apostrophe (') is after the *s* in *guests* because more than one guest is using the tables. If only one guest is using the tables, the phrase would be *the guest's tables.* How would you write "socks that belong to more than one girl"?

CONTENT CONNECTION

The servers at Candy's serve food to earn money. What jobs do you do to earn money? Do you earn money for doing jobs at home?

After You Read

A. Applying the Math

Can you plan a party on a budget? Imagine that you need to plan a birthday party for 20 guests. You have a $400 budget. You also have a list of items, services, and costs from Kim's Caterers. Complete the following budget chart to show what you want from Kim's and how much it will cost. You already know that you want cake and ice cream for everyone.

Kim's Caterers Party List

- Full meal with servers: $15 per guest
- Cake and ice cream: $5 per guest
- Water and juices: $2.50 per guest
- Water, juices, and sodas: $3.00 per guest
- Music played on a stereo system: $75
- Music played by a live band: $175

- Balloons and *Happy Birthday* signs: $50
- Balloons, *Happy Birthday* signs, party lights, and a dance floor: $100
- Movies, popcorn, and snacks: $5 per guest
- Games and sports equipment: $5 per guest
- Photographer and book of pictures: $75

My Party Budget

Total Amount to Spend: _____ $400 _____

Number of Guests: _____ 20 _____

Item	Cost	Total
Cake and ice cream	$5 per guest × 20 guests	$100

Total Cost: _____

Amount Under or Over Budget: _____

How did the budget chart help you plan your party? Was it easy to stay within your budget? Write two or more sentences to answer these questions. Would you use a budget chart again? Why or why not?

_____

_____

B. Comprehension Skills

Tip! **Think about how to find answers.** Read each sentence below. Underline the words that will help you figure out how to complete each item.

Mark box **a, b,** or **c** with an **X** before the choice that best completes each sentence.

Recalling Facts

1. Caterers provide
- ☐ **a.** food and services for events.
- ☐ **b.** budgets for special events.
- ☐ **c.** reasons to have large parties.

2. People who hire caterers usually
- ☐ **a.** ask what type of food will be served to the guests.
- ☐ **b.** charge the caterer for party items.
- ☐ **c.** set a budget for the entire event.

3. A budget is
- ☐ **a.** the least amount of money that an event will cost.
- ☐ **b.** a plan to use a certain amount of money.
- ☐ **c.** the total cost of a party.

4. The Apex budget would not allow for both
- ☐ **a.** key chain hammers and a buffet.
- ☐ **b.** a choice of desserts and a buffet.
- ☐ **c.** key chain hammers and servers.

5. Caterers' budgets include money
- ☐ **a.** to pay the people who host the event.
- ☐ **b.** to buy gifts for servers.
- ☐ **c.** to hire servers.

Understanding Ideas

1. From the article, you can conclude that
- ☐ **a.** the caterer's budget is not as important as the host's budget.
- ☐ **b.** it is important to decide on a budget before you plan an event.
- ☐ **c.** it is best to change the budget when plans do not work.

2. You can also conclude that a person who "works within a budget" probably
- ☐ **a.** spends more than the budget allows.
- ☐ **b.** adds more money to the budget.
- ☐ **c.** makes changes to cut costs.

3. Candy's could suggest that Apex use the extra $450 in the budget to
- ☐ **a.** purchase more of Candy's services.
- ☐ **b.** give big tips to the servers.
- ☐ **c.** give some money to each guest.

4. It is most likely true that Apex
- ☐ **a.** will not use Candy's for future events.
- ☐ **b.** will always choose the buffet for future events.
- ☐ **c.** thought it was important to give key chain hammers to the new workers.

5. Candy's probably pays servers
- ☐ **a.** from the money it charges for its services.
- ☐ **b.** less than other caterers pay servers.
- ☐ **c.** from the money saved by using buffets.

C. Reading Strategies

1. Recognizing Words in Context

Find the word *additional* in the article. One definition below is closest to the meaning of that word. One definition has the opposite or nearly the opposite meaning. The remaining definition has a meaning that has nothing to do with the word. Label the definitions **C** for *closest*, **O** for *opposite* or *nearly opposite*, and **U** for *unrelated*.

_____ **a.** less

_____ **b.** last

_____ **c.** more

2. Distinguishing Fact from Opinion

Two of the statements below present *facts,* which can be proved. The other statement is an *opinion,* which expresses someone's thoughts or beliefs. Label the statements **F** for *fact* and **O** for *opinion.*

_____ **a.** Caterers sometimes provide services other than food.

_____ **b.** Caterers make it easier to plan an event.

_____ **c.** A budget lets caterers know how much people want to spend.

3. Making Correct Inferences

Two of the statements below are correct *inferences,* or reasonable guesses, that are based on information in the article. The other statement is an incorrect inference. Label the statements **C** for *correct* inference and **I** for *incorrect* inference.

_____ **a.** People may hire caterers when they do not have time to host an event by themselves.

_____ **b.** To stay within a budget, people may have to adjust their plans.

_____ **c.** It always costs people more money to pay a caterer than to buy their own food.

4. Understanding Main Ideas

One of the statements below expresses the main idea of the article. Another statement is too general, or too broad. The other explains only part of the article; it is too narrow. Label the statements **M** for *main idea,* **B** for *too broad,* and **N** for *too narrow.*

_____ **a.** Caterers help people host events.

_____ **b.** People hire caterers to help with events, and they use budgets to plan the best use of their money.

_____ **c.** Sometimes people make adjustments to stay within their budgets.

5. Responding to the Article

Complete the following sentence in your own words:

From reading "Catering an Event," I have learned

_____

_____

D. Expanding Vocabulary

Content-Area Words

Read each item carefully. Write on the line the word that best completes each sentence.

1. Someone who decides to host a meeting has to _____ it.
   attend   plan   forget

2. I hired caterers to bring food because my guests will be _____.
   bored   late   hungry

3. Kim's _____ is an event that I do not want to miss.
   book   party   garden

4. Because the _____ was not good, he made adjustments to the recipe.
   cake   shirt   apple

5. The budget helped John decide how to use his _____.
   bike   fork   money

Academic English

In the article "Catering an Event," you learned that *selection* means "a group of things to choose from." *Selection* can also mean "a person or thing that is chosen," as in the following sentence.

   The students have made their selection for the new class president.

Complete the sentence below.

1. My favorite *selection* on the breakfast menu is _____

Now use the word *selection* in a sentence of your own.

2. _____

You also learned that *final* is an adjective that means "last" or "at the end of something." *Final* can also be a noun that means "the last game or match in a contest," as in the following sentence.

   I hope our team is in the soccer final at the end of the season.

Complete the sentence below.

3. The team that wins the contest *final* will receive a _____

Now use the word *final* in two sentences of your own.

4. _____

5. _____

 Share your new sentences with a partner.

Before You Read

 Think about what you know. Skim the article on the opposite page. How are you connected to other people? Do you know people outside your family? Do people in your family know anyone that you do not know?

Vocabulary

The content-area and academic English words below appear in "Small-World Theory." Read the definitions and the example sentences.

Content-Area Words

connected (kə nek′tid) joined or linked together
   Example: Asha is *connected* to her grandparents through her parents.

separation (sep′ə rā′shən) distance or gap between two things
   Example: A river can be a natural *separation* between cities or states.

assumes (ə soomz′) considers something to be a fact without knowing it for certain
   Example: My team *assumes* that the game will be canceled if it rains.

proved (proovd) showed something to be true
   Example: My experiment *proved* that plants grow better when people talk to them.

networks (net′wurks′) groups or systems of things that are linked in some way
   Example: People have *networks* of friends at school and at work.

Academic English

theory (thē′ər ē) an idea that may be true but that no one has showed to be true
   Example: Shahaf agrees with the *theory* that there may be life on other planets.

establish (es tab′lish) to show that something exists or is true
   Example: Before we plan a party, we must *establish* that people can come.

Read again the example sentences that follow the content-area and academic English word definitions. With a partner, discuss the meanings of the words and sentences.

 Now skim the article and look for other words that are new to you. Write each new word and its definition in the Personal Dictionary.

While You Read

 Think about why you read. Have you ever learned that you were connected to someone you thought you did not know? How were you connected to the person? As you read, look for the main idea about how people are connected.

1 Each year Ben is glad when school is closed on Martin Luther King Jr. Day. Ben knows that this day honors an important man, but Ben does not feel **connected** to him. However, the *small-world **theory*** links Ben to Dr. King. Ben's mom (0) has a stepfather (1). The stepfather's uncle (2) once met and spoke to
5 Eleanor Mondale (3), the daughter of former Vice President Walter Mondale (4). Walter Mondale knew Dr. King (5). In a way, Ben is only "five people away" from Martin Luther King Jr.

The small-world theory states that everyone in the world is connected through a short chain of people they know. Another name for this chain is *degrees of*
10 *separation.* Each degree is a step that separates a person from someone he or she does not know. There are zero degrees of separation between a person and the people he or she knows directly. This means that there are zero degrees between Ben and his mom. There is one degree of separation when just one person separates someone from a person he or she does not know. Ben knows his mom,
15 but he has never met her stepfather. Therefore, Ben is one degree away from the stepfather. As the chain continues, the stepfather's uncle is two degrees. Eleanor Mondale is three degrees, and her father is four degrees. Dr. King is five degrees away from Ben. The theory states that there are no more than six degrees of separation between any two people in the world.

20 The small-world theory is based on math. The theory **assumes** that each person knows 100 people. Each one of those 100 people knows 50 different people. Each of those 50 people knows another 50 people, and so on. When someone continues the calculation to six degrees, it multiplies like this: $100 \times 50 \times 50 \times 50 \times 50 \times 50 = 31.25 \times 10^9$. This number is greater than 31 billion. There are over 6 billion
25 people in the world. These numbers show it is possible that six degrees of separation could include everyone in the world.

Does the small-world theory work? No one has ever **proved** it. Some people have questions about how well it works in certain areas. For example, the theory needs to **establish** links to groups of people in distant places, such as jungles or
30 deserts. The theory may not work in places where most people know only the other people in their village. Also, the theory depends on a few people with large **networks** who link everybody else together.

Does the theory matter to people? Maybe it just makes people think a little more about their places in the world.

LANGUAGE CONNECTION

A metaphor compares two objects or ideas without using the words *like* or *as*. Explain what the metaphor *chain of people* means.

CONTENT CONNECTION

There were approximately 6,515,598,712 people in the world in April 2005. Do you think you are connected to this many people by only six degrees of separation? Is there anyone that you do not think you could be connected to?

After You Read

A. Applying the Math

How many degrees separate you from other people? Complete the bubble chart below. Think about someone who is connected to you by at least three degrees of separation. Fill in the chart to show the degrees of separation. Think of each bubble as one degree. In each bubble, underline the name or the title of the next person in the connection. An example has been done for you.

Example: **My Chart:**

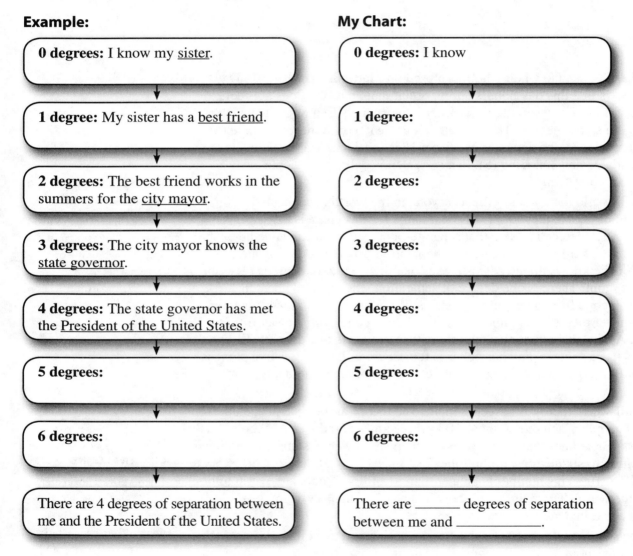

0 degrees: I know my <u>sister</u>.

1 degree: My sister has a <u>best friend</u>.

2 degrees: The best friend works in the summers for the <u>city mayor</u>.

3 degrees: The city mayor knows the <u>state governor</u>.

4 degrees: The state governor has met the <u>President of the United States</u>.

5 degrees:

6 degrees:

There are 4 degrees of separation between me and the President of the United States.

0 degrees: I know

1 degree:

2 degrees:

3 degrees:

4 degrees:

5 degrees:

6 degrees:

There are _____ degrees of separation between me and _____.

Did completing the chart help you see how you are connected to other people? Do you agree with the theory that you could be connected to anyone in the world by six degrees or less? Write two or more sentences to answer these questions.

_____

_____

B. Comprehension Skills

 Think about how to find answers. Look back at different parts of the text. What facts help you figure out how to complete the sentences?

Mark box **a, b,** or **c** with an **X** before the choice that best completes each sentence.

Recalling Facts

1. The small-world theory states that no more than six degrees separate
   - ☐ **a.** members of a family.
   - ☐ **b.** any two people in the world.
   - ☐ **c.** students and their classmates.

2. The number of degrees of separation between Lee and her friend Ami is
   - ☐ **a.** one.
   - ☐ **b.** zero.
   - ☐ **c.** three.

3. The number of degrees of separation between Lee and Ami's aunt is
   - ☐ **a.** one.
   - ☐ **b.** two.
   - ☐ **c.** three.

4. Ben is three degrees away from
   - ☐ **a.** Eleanor Mondale.
   - ☐ **b.** his mom's dentist.
   - ☐ **c.** Dr. Martin Luther King Jr.

5. The small-world theory assumes that each person knows
   - ☐ **a.** 6 people.
   - ☐ **b.** 50 people.
   - ☐ **c.** 100 people.

Understanding Ideas

1. From the article, you can conclude that
   - ☐ **a.** the small-world theory works.
   - ☐ **b.** everyone knows 100 people.
   - ☐ **c.** more research may or may not prove the small-world theory.

2. Famous people probably have
   - ☐ **a.** more degrees of separation between them and others.
   - ☐ **b.** fewer degrees of separation between them and others.
   - ☐ **c.** zero degrees of separation between them and others.

3. The small-world theory may not work very well with
   - ☐ **a.** movie actors.
   - ☐ **b.** people who live in distant places.
   - ☐ **c.** government workers.

4. Eleanor Mondale is one degree away from
   - ☐ **a.** Ben.
   - ☐ **b.** Walter Mondale.
   - ☐ **c.** Dr. Martin Luther King Jr.

5. If Ben's mom's doctor knows Britney's doctor, then Ben is
   - ☐ **a.** three degrees away from Britney.
   - ☐ **b.** four degrees away from Britney.
   - ☐ **c.** five degrees away from Britney.

C. Reading Strategies

1. Recognizing Words in Context

Find the word *distant* in the article. One definition below is closest to the meaning of that word. One definition has the opposite or nearly the opposite meaning. The remaining definition has a meaning that has nothing to do with the word. Label the definitions **C** for *closest*, **O** for *opposite* or *nearly opposite*, and **U** for *unrelated*.

_____ **a.** far

_____ **b.** close

_____ **c.** noisy

2. Distinguishing Fact from Opinion

Two of the statements below present *facts,* which can be proved. The other statement is an *opinion,* which expresses someone's thoughts or beliefs. Label the statements **F** for *fact* and **O** for *opinion.*

_____ **a.** There are zero degrees of separation between two friends.

_____ **b.** Scientists have not proved the small-world theory.

_____ **c.** The small-world theory cannot work in distant places.

3. Making Correct Inferences

Two of the statements below are correct *inferences,* or reasonable guesses, that are based on information in the article. The other statement is an incorrect inference. Label the statements **C** for *correct* inference and **I** for *incorrect* inference.

_____ **a.** The small-world theory assumes things that may not be true for everyone.

_____ **b.** People with larger networks are connected to fewer people.

_____ **c.** People can be connected to people they do not know.

4. Understanding Main Ideas

One of the statements below expresses the main idea of the article. Another statement is too general, or too broad. The other explains only part of the article; it is too narrow. Label the statements **M** for *main idea,* **B** for *too broad,* and **N** for *too narrow.*

_____ **a.** There are zero degrees of separation between two people who know each other.

_____ **b.** The small-world theory says that people are connected to other people.

_____ **c.** The small-world theory states that no more than six degrees separate any two people.

5. Responding to the Article

Complete the following sentence in your own words:

Reading "Small-World Theory" made me want to learn more about

_____

because _____

_____

While You Read

 Think about why you read. Have you ever wondered how race cars go so fast? When people build race cars, what kinds of things must they consider? As you read, try to find the answer.

Race Cars
Behind the Speed

1   Race cars are some of the fastest machines in the world. An Indy-style race car is the kind of car that races at the Indianapolis 500, a famous car race. Indy-style cars can reach speeds above 230 miles per hour. That is faster than many small planes can fly.

5   Race cars must be able to change direction often. For this reason, race teams need to **compute** the **velocity** of a car as well as its speed. Velocity is the rate at which something moves in a certain direction. Speed also tells people how fast an object moves, but it does not tell how the object has changed position. To figure speed, divide distance by time. For example, imagine that you drive 140
10 miles in two hours, and that you travel west. Your speed is 70 miles per hour (140 ÷ 2 = 70 mph). However, your velocity is 70 miles per hour *west*.

  Now imagine that Jenny drives at 70 miles per hour to the next town. She returns home at the same speed. This means that, on **average,** her speed is 70 miles per hour. However, her average velocity is zero, because she has not actually
15 changed her position. Jenny has returned to the same point from which she started.

  Friction is a force that can lower the speed and velocity of a car. Friction slows down motion. As a race car moves, its tires roll and rub against the track. This causes friction.

  Engineers are people who have the skills to build things. Some engineers
20 **design** race cars. They study the **coefficient** of friction. To find the coefficient of friction for an object, a person must know both the weight of the object and the force needed to move the object. Imagine that you need to use 20 pounds of force to push a 100-pound box across a floor. To compute the coefficient of friction, you divide 20 by 100. The coefficient of friction for the box is .2.
25 Objects that have oil on them, such as race car wheels and machine parts, have much lower coefficients of friction. Their coefficients of friction are usually about .002.

  The science of **aerodynamics** studies the ways that friction from air affects the motion of objects. As a race car passes through air, forces push against it. People
30 who design race cars study these forces to help their cars perform better. Drag is air friction that forces a car to slow down. Downward forces help hold the car on the track. When a car has more force holding it on the track, it can go faster around corners and through curves. People who design race cars try to make the drag on a car lower and the downward forces on the car higher.

CONTENT CONNECTION

The people who built the Indianapolis Motor Speedway planned it as a place to test new cars. Then they decided that once each year they would use it for a 500-mile car race. In 1911 the first Indianapolis 500 took place. Would you like to go to this race? Why or why not?

LANGUAGE CONNECTION

A homophone is a word that sounds the same as another word but has a different meaning. Look at the noun *weight*. The verb *wait* sounds the same as *weight*. Can you use *wait* in a sentence?

After You Read

A. Organizing Ideas

How do forces affect the speed and velocity of race cars? Complete the chart below. Fill in the names and definitions of three forces that affect how fast race cars can travel. Then write sentences to explain how the forces affect the cars. Use information from the article to help you. Some have been done for you.

Force	Definition	How It Affects Race Cars
friction		
		This force occurs because cars travel through air. It causes cars to slow down.
	forces that hold down a car	

What did you learn about the forces that affect how fast race cars can travel? What forces help cars go faster or make cars slow down? Write two or more sentences to answer these questions. How did the chart help you answer the questions?

_____

_____

_____

_____

_____

B. Comprehension Skills

 Think about how to find answers. Look back at what you read. The information is in the text, but you may have to look in several sentences to find it.

Mark box **a, b,** or **c** with an **X** before the choice that best completes each sentence.

Recalling Facts

1. Race cars in the Indianapolis 500 can reach speeds of more than
   ☐ **a.** 230 miles per hour.
   ☐ **b.** 200 miles per hour.
   ☐ **c.** 185 miles per hour.

2. The rate at which something moves in a certain direction is its
   ☐ **a.** speed.
   ☐ **b.** velocity.
   ☐ **c.** downward force.

3. A force that slows down motion is
   ☐ **a.** friction.
   ☐ **b.** velocity.
   ☐ **c.** a car tire.

4. The science that studies the way air affects the motion of objects is
   ☐ **a.** friction.
   ☐ **b.** drag forces.
   ☐ **c.** aerodynamics.

5. To compute the coefficient of friction, engineers
   ☐ **a.** make the downward forces high.
   ☐ **b.** add the weight of an object and the force needed to move it.
   ☐ **c.** divide the force needed to move an object by the weight of the object.

Understanding Ideas

1. From the article, you can conclude that people who design race cars
   ☐ **a.** will start to build heavier cars.
   ☐ **b.** want to design faster cars.
   ☐ **c.** have improved aerodynamics as much as possible.

2. You can also conclude that strong drag forces will probably
   ☐ **a.** cause a race car to stop.
   ☐ **b.** cause a race car to go faster.
   ☐ **c.** cause a race car to go slower.

3. A chair that Lulu pushes across a wood floor probably has a lower coefficient of friction than
   ☐ **a.** a desk that she pushes across a rug.
   ☐ **b.** a ball that she rolls on the ground.
   ☐ **c.** the blades of her ice skates as they move on the ice.

4. A ball that rolls across the floor will stop because
   ☐ **a.** of friction.
   ☐ **b.** someone did not push it hard enough.
   ☐ **c.** downward forces pull it down.

5. Without drag, race cars would move
   ☐ **a.** slowly.
   ☐ **b.** faster than they do.
   ☐ **c.** at different speeds from one another.

C. Reading Strategies

1. Recognizing Words in Context

Find the word *perform* in the article. One definition below is closest to the meaning of that word. One definition has the opposite or nearly the opposite meaning. The remaining definition has a meaning that has nothing to do with the word. Label the definitions **C** for *closest*, **O** for *opposite* or *nearly opposite*, and **U** for *unrelated*.

_____ **a.** fail

_____ **b.** change

_____ **c.** work

2. Distinguishing Fact from Opinion

Two of the statements below present *facts*, which can be proved. The other statement is an *opinion*, which expresses someone's thoughts or beliefs. Label the statements **F** for *fact* and **O** for *opinion*.

_____ **a.** Velocity is more important to engineers than speed.

_____ **b.** The velocity of a car includes the direction of movement.

_____ **c.** Drag occurs when air friction slows down a car.

3. Making Correct Inferences

Two of the statements below are correct *inferences,* or reasonable guesses, that are based on information in the article. The other statement is an incorrect inference. Label the statements **C** for *correct* inference and **I** for *incorrect* inference.

_____ **a.** The car that travels at the fastest speed does not always win the race.

_____ **b.** Cars would race better without any friction at all on the track.

_____ **c.** Car designers must know a great deal about cars and aerodynamics.

4. Understanding Main Ideas

One of the statements below expresses the main idea of the article. Another statement is too general, or too broad. The other explains only part of the article; it is too narrow. Label the statements **M** for *main idea*, **B** for *too broad*, and **N** for *too narrow*.

_____ **a.** Race car designers must consider the forces that affect the speed and velocity of a car.

_____ **b.** Engineers who design cars must study many different forces.

_____ **c.** Aerodynamics is the science that studies how air friction affects moving objects.

5. Responding to the Article

Complete the following sentence in your own words:

One thing in "Race Cars: Behind the Speed" that I cannot understand is

_____

_____

D. Expanding Vocabulary

Content-Area Words

Complete each sentence with a word from the box. Write the missing word on the line.

velocity	average	friction	coefficient	aerodynamics

1. To make the drag on a car lower, engineers must understand _____.

2. A person must add and divide to find the _____ of a set of numbers.

3. An object that rubs against another object will be affected by _____.

4. Lower the _____ of friction to make something easier to push.

5. The girl rode her bike at a _____ of 10 miles per hour north.

Academic English

In the article "Race Cars: Behind the Speed," you learned that *compute* means "to calculate an amount or a number." *Compute* can describe what people do when they make calculations in many different situations, as in the following sentence.

She cannot compute the gas mileage until she knows how far the car has traveled.

Complete the sentence below.

1. Teachers look at test scores when they *compute* a student's final _____

Now use the word *compute* in a sentence of your own.

2. _____

_____

You also learned that *design* is a verb that means "to use skills to plan the parts and details of something." *Design* can also be a noun that means "a plan or sketch that people can use as a guide or pattern for building something," as in the following sentence.

The engineer showed us pictures of his new car design.

Complete the sentence below.

3. The builder will create a *design* for the _____

Now use the word *design* in two sentences of your own.

4. _____

5. _____

 Share your new sentences with a partner.

Roman Numerals

Before You Read

 Think about what you know. Read the lesson title above. What do you think the article will be about? Have you ever heard of Roman numerals?

Vocabulary

The content-area and academic English words below appear in "Roman Numerals." Read the definitions and the example sentences.

Content-Area Words

ancient (ān'shənt) related to times that were long ago
   Example: I like learning about the people who lived in *ancient* Greece.

system (sis'təm) a group of things that combine to form one larger group or whole
   Example: The Roman numeral *system* helped Romans do business.

numerals (noo'mər əlz) symbols that represent numbers
   Example: The numbers on my watch are Roman *numerals*.

records (rek'ərdz) information that people write down and save
   Example: Doctors keep *records* about the health of their patients.

arrange (ə rānj') to put things in a certain order
   Example: The teacher will *arrange* the student desks in five rows.

Academic English

feature (fē'chər) a part of something
   Example: Headlights are an important *feature* of a car.

constructed (kən strukt'əd) built; put together
   Example: The builders *constructed* the new school in only 10 months.

Answer the questions below about the content-area and academic English words. Write your answers in the spaces provided. The first one has been done for you.

1. What word goes with *grades that teachers write down in a book?* _____records_____

2. What word goes with *put names in alphabetical order?* _____

3. What word goes with *old Greek statues in a museum?* _____

4. What word goes with *a group with different parts?* _____

5. What word goes with *the seat of a bike?* _____

6. What word goes with *six is 6 and five is 5?* _____

7. What word goes with *builder, bricks, nails, and wood?* _____

Dictionary Now skim the article and look for other words that are new to you. Write each new word and its definition in the Personal Dictionary.

While You Read

 Think about why you read. Where have you seen Roman numerals before? Do you know how to read them when you see them? As you read, look for information about how to find the value of a Roman numeral.

Roman Numerals

1   The Romans, the **ancient** people of Rome in Italy, created the Roman number **system.** The ancient Greeks needed to use numbers for theories in areas such as geometry and physics. However, the Romans did not develop these types of theories. They created their numbers for different reasons. The Romans used their
5   numbers mostly to do business. Romans also used the **numerals** to keep **records** of taxes and trade. These records were important because Rome ruled a very large empire that included countries throughout the world.

The Romans used numerals that are the same as some of the letters in the alphabet. The numerals I, V, X, L, C, D, and M stand for 1, 5, 10, 50, 100, 500,
10   and 1,000. To write a large number in Roman numerals, a person must **arrange** the single number values from left to right. The greatest value goes on the left, and the smallest value goes on the right. To find the value of the entire number, a person adds together all of the single number values. For example, a person would read the number MDCLXVI as 1,000 + 500 + 100 + 50 + 10 + 5 + 1, or 1,666.

15   Some numbers include the same numeral more than once. The number 8 is VIII. A person adds three Is to V to equal 8. If numbers with lower values are on the right side of a higher number, a person adds the lower numbers to the higher number. The number VIII, then, is 5 + 1 + 1 + 1 = 8.

Except for very large numbers, Romans never used the same numeral more
20   than three times in a row. They did not write the number 4 as IIII. Instead they used subtraction. If a number with a lower value is on the left side of a higher number, then a person subtracts the lower number from the higher number. Four is 5 minus 1, or IV. Nine is 10 minus 1, or IX. Forty is 50 minus 10, or XL.

The subtraction **feature** of Roman numerals may make it difficult to figure out
25   the values of some numbers that have three numerals in them. For example, XIX is 19, or 10 + 9. Why does XIX not equal 21, or 10 + 1 + 10? The subtraction rule means that IX stands for 9. So XIX is 10 (X) plus 9 (IX). You add the larger number to the smaller number that comes after it. This equals 19. The numeral for 21 is XXI.

30   People still use Roman numerals today, but not very often. Roman numerals that are carved into a corner of some large buildings show the year when people **constructed** the buildings. Roman numerals are also on the faces of some clocks and watches. Sometimes Roman numerals are the page numbers for the first pages of books.

LANGUAGE CONNECTION

Theories is the plural of *theory.* For many nouns that end in *y,* the *y* changes to *ies* to form the plural. What is the plural of *activity? Baby? Day?*

CONTENT CONNECTION

The Roman numeral C stands for 100, and V stands for 5. Can you find the value of the Roman numeral VC? Would CV have a different value or the same value?

After You Read

A. Organizing Ideas

What have you learned about Roman numerals? Complete the outline below. Write on the lines the facts that you learned from the article. Some have been done for you.

The Roman Numeral System

I. History of the Roman numeral system
   A. _Created by ancient Romans_
   B. _____
   C. _____

II. How to write a Roman numeral
   A. _I, V, X, L, C, D, and M stand for_
   B. _The greatest value goes on the_
   C. _____

III. How to find the value of a Roman numeral
   A. _Add together the_
   B. _If a lower numeral is on the right side of a higher numeral,_
   _____
   _____
   C. _____
   _____

IV. Where we see Roman numerals today
   A. _On large buildings_
   B. _____
   C. _____
   D. _In outlines!_

What do you know about Roman numerals? Write two or more sentences to explain facts that you learned from the article. Did the outline help you see what you have learned about Roman numerals? Why or why not?

_____

_____

B. Comprehension Skills

Tip! **Think about how to find answers.** Think about what each sentence means. Try to say it to yourself in your own words before you complete it.

Mark box **a, b,** or **c** with an **X** before the choice that best completes each sentence.

Recalling Facts

1. The ancient Romans used numerals
   - ☐ **a.** for business purposes.
   - ☐ **b.** in Roman geometry theories.
   - ☐ **c.** because they admired the ancient Greeks.

2. To write a large Roman numeral, put the greater values
   - ☐ **a.** on the left.
   - ☐ **b.** on the right.
   - ☐ **c.** in the middle.

3. To find the value of the Roman numeral MDCLXVI,
   - ☐ **a.** subtract all of the values from M.
   - ☐ **b.** add the single number values together.
   - ☐ **c.** count the number of values.

4. To show the number 40 in Roman numerals, the Romans
   - ☐ **a.** added four 10s.
   - ☐ **b.** added two 20s.
   - ☐ **c.** subtracted 10 from 50.

5. To find the value of the Roman numeral IX,
   - ☐ **a.** add the larger number to the smaller number.
   - ☐ **b.** subtract the smaller number from the larger number.
   - ☐ **c.** subtract the larger number from the smaller number.

Understanding Ideas

1. One word that describes the way that the Romans used math is
   - ☐ **a.** *proud.*
   - ☐ **b.** *artistic.*
   - ☐ **c.** *businesslike.*

2. The Roman number system was probably
   - ☐ **a.** used only in Rome.
   - ☐ **b.** taught to Romans by the Greeks.
   - ☐ **c.** used throughout the Roman Empire.

3. In Roman numerals, the number 89 is
   - ☐ **a.** LIX.
   - ☐ **b.** XIX.
   - ☐ **c.** LXXXIX.

4. From the article, you can conclude that the year 2007 in Roman numerals is
   - ☐ **a.** MMVII.
   - ☐ **b.** MDLX.
   - ☐ **c.** MMIIV.

5. You can also conclude that it is not true that
   - ☐ **a.** the Roman numeral for zero is 0.
   - ☐ **b.** sometimes people use Roman numerals today.
   - ☐ **c.** a person uses addition and subtraction to understand Roman numerals.

C. Reading Strategies

1. Recognizing Words in Context

Find the word *empire* in the article. One definition below is closest to the meaning of that word. One definition has the opposite or nearly the opposite meaning. The remaining definition has a meaning that has nothing to do with the word. Label the definitions **C** for *closest*, **O** for *opposite* or *nearly opposite*, and **U** for *unrelated*.

_____ **a.** kingdom

_____ **b.** town

_____ **c.** jewel

2. Distinguishing Fact from Opinion

Two of the statements below present *facts*, which can be proved. The other statement is an *opinion*, which expresses someone's thoughts or beliefs. Label the statements **F** for *fact* and **O** for *opinion*.

_____ **a.** The order of the numerals is important in a Roman numeral.

_____ **b.** The Roman numeral for 22 is XXII.

_____ **c.** Roman numerals are more difficult to read than the numbers of other systems.

3. Making Correct Inferences

Two of the statements below are correct *inferences*, or reasonable guesses, that are based on information in the article. The other statement is an incorrect inference. Label the statements **C** for *correct* inference and **I** for *incorrect* inference.

_____ **a.** Many people today do not know how to read Roman numerals.

_____ **b.** Roman numerals appear more often on older things.

_____ **c.** The Romans did not need a number system.

4. Understanding Main Ideas

One of the statements below expresses the main idea of the article. Another statement is too general, or too broad. The other explains only part of the article; it is too narrow. Label the statements **M** for *main idea*, **B** for *too broad*, and **N** for *too narrow*.

_____ **a.** People must add and subtract to write and read Roman numerals.

_____ **b.** It can be difficult to read Roman numbers with three numerals.

_____ **c.** Romans created an important number system long ago.

5. Responding to the Article

Complete the following sentences in your own words:

One of the things I did best while reading "Roman Numerals" was

_____

I think that I did this well because _____

_____

D. Expanding Vocabulary

Content-Area Words

Complete each analogy with a word from the box. Write in the missing word.

ancient	system	numerals	records	arrange

1. twist : spin :: organize : _____

2. *m, y* : letters :: *5, 7* : _____

3. throw away : garbage :: keep : _____

4. bones : body :: parts : _____

5. good : bad :: new : _____

Academic English

In the article "Roman Numerals," you learned that *feature* is a noun that means "a part of something." *Feature* can also be a verb that means "to include something as an important part," as in the following sentence.

   The movie will feature one of my favorite actors.

Complete the sentence below.

1. A child's birthday party would *feature* _____

Now use the word *feature* in a sentence of your own.

2. _____

_____

You also learned that *constructed* means "built" or "put together." *Constructed* can describe the action of people who build or put together things with their hands. *Constructed* can also describe the action of people who build or put together things in their minds, as in the following sentence.

   Our team constructed a plan to win the championship.

Complete the sentence below.

3. When the teacher asked me a question, I quickly *constructed* an _____

Now use the word *constructed* in two sentences of your own.

4. _____

5. _____

 Share your new sentences with a partner.

Before You Read

 Think about what you know. Skim the article on the opposite page. Think about what you know about borrowing money. Have you ever let someone borrow money from you?

Vocabulary

The content-area and academic English words below appear in "The Business of Borrowing Money." Read the definitions and the example sentences.

Content-Area Words

mortgage (môr′gij) a loan that people use to buy a house
   Example: After 20 years of *mortgage* payments, Mr. Garcia owns his house.

lend (lend) to allow someone to use an item and then return it
   Example: Yoko will *lend* me her sweater if I take good care of it.

credit (kred′it) trust or confidence that a person can repay a loan or pay a bill
   Example: Donnell established good *credit* by always paying his bills on time.

profit (prof′it) the money that remains after a business has paid all of its costs
   Example: We made a *profit* of $150 when we sold snacks at the soccer game.

interest (in′trist) money that a customer pays to borrow money from a lender
   Example: My aunt explained that she must pay *interest* on her car loan.

Academic English

available (ə vā′lə bəl) ready to have or to use
   Example: The shoes are not *available* in my size at this store.

factors (fak′tərz) things that cause results or that are important parts in a situation
   Example: The low price of the book was one of the *factors* that made me buy it.

Read again the example sentences that follow the content-area and academic English word definitions. With a partner, discuss the meanings of the words and sentences.

Dictionary Now skim the article and look for other words that are new to you. Write each new word and its definition in the Personal Dictionary.

While You Read

Tip! **Think about why you read.** What do you need to do if you want a bank to give you a loan? Write down a question about borrowing money that you would like to know the answer to. As you read, you may find the answer.

THE BUSINESS OF
Borrowing Money

1　People who want to buy an expensive item, such as a car, probably need to borrow money, or get a loan, from a bank. When someone wants to buy a house, that person needs a long-term loan called a *mortgage*. Banks **lend** money to people who have paid their bills on time. When people pay bills on time, they
5　establish good **credit.** Lenders, or people who lend money, examine the credit histories of customers to decide whether they want to lend money to the customers. A credit history is a record that shows how much money a person owes and whether that person has been paying his or her bills on time.

　　A lender also wants to know how much a borrower earns each month. This
10　helps a bank to decide if the borrower is able to repay a loan. For example, imagine that a customer applies for a car loan. Every month that person earns $1,200. The customer has monthly credit card payments of $175 and monthly rent payments of $500. This information means the customer has $525 left over for other monthly costs. The bank needs to decide whether the customer can pay
15　a $260 car payment each month.

　　Banks and other lenders, such as mortgage companies, make a **profit** when they lend money. They make money when they charge people **interest.** The amount of interest they charge is the interest rate. It is a percentage of the loan amount. Imagine that a customer gets a $10,000 loan with an interest rate of 7
20　percent. The customer needs to pay back a total of $10,700 to the lender. Some banks offer lower interest rates than others. They may do this especially for customers who have good credit histories. That is because banks believe that people with good credit are more likely to repay a loan than people with poor credit. It is a good idea to look at different banks and companies in order to find
25　the best interest rate **available.** For example, imagine that you borrow $10,000 to buy a car. Your interest rate is 7 percent, and you need to repay the loan in three years. If you get an interest rate of 3 percent instead, your monthly payment is about $18 lower.

　　Banks and other companies that lend money must borrow money from the
30　Federal Reserve Bank. This bank decides the rate of interest that it will charge other banks. People call this rate the *prime rate*. It affects the amount of interest the other banks charge. The amount a person has to pay to borrow money depends on three major **factors.** These factors are the prime rate, the credit history of the person, and competition among lenders.

LANGUAGE CONNECTION

Symbols are letters or figures that represent something. The $ symbol stands for the word *dollars*. So *$5* means "five dollars." Do you know what the % symbol stands for?

CONTENT CONNECTION

Isabel has a $100 credit card payment each month, and she has never paid it late. Jamal has a $250 credit card payment each month. Last year he paid it late three times. If you worked at a bank, would you rather loan money to Isabel or to Jamal? Why?

After You Read

A. Organizing Ideas

What do borrowers and lenders do? Complete the chart below. In the left column, write down what borrowers must do when they want a loan. In the right column, write down what lenders must do to decide whether or not to give the loan. Use the article to find information. You may also include your own ideas. Some have been done for you.

Before they ask for a loan, borrowers must	Before they give a loan, lenders must
• consider how much money they need to borrow to make the purchase.	• examine credit history to see if the borrower pays bills on time.
• _____	• _____
• _____	• decide whether the borrower can afford to repay the loan.
• check the prime rate from the Federal Reserve Bank.	• _____
• _____	• _____

Do you think it is easy or difficult to get a loan from a bank? Write two or more sentences to explain your answer. Did the chart help you reach this conclusion? Why or why not?

_____

_____

_____

B. Comprehension Skills

 Think about how to find answers. Look back at what you read. The words in an answer are usually contained in a single sentence.

Mark box **a, b,** or **c** with an **X** before the choice that best completes each sentence.

Recalling Facts

1. A loan for a home is a
   - ☐ **a.** mortgage.
   - ☐ **b.** prime rate.
   - ☐ **c.** rate of interest.

2. Banks are most likely to lend money to people
   - ☐ **a.** who have a mortgage.
   - ☐ **b.** with good credit histories.
   - ☐ **c.** who have borrowed money from them before.

3. Banks make a profit from
   - ☐ **a.** interest on loans.
   - ☐ **b.** the sale of houses.
   - ☐ **c.** interest on savings accounts.

4. The prime rate
   - ☐ **a.** does not affect other interest rates.
   - ☐ **b.** is the interest rate set by the Federal Reserve Bank.
   - ☐ **c.** is the interest rate that banks offer to customers with good credit.

5. It is not true that
   - ☐ **a.** the Federal Reserve Bank can lower the prime rate.
   - ☐ **b.** the prime rate affects the amount of interest that banks charge.
   - ☐ **c.** the Federal Reserve Bank decides how much money other banks can lend.

Understanding Ideas

1. Before a bank lends money to a person, it looks at the person's
   - ☐ **a.** credit history.
   - ☐ **b.** monthly earnings.
   - ☐ **c.** credit history and monthly earnings.

2. Banks compete with one another by offering
   - ☐ **a.** mortgage loans.
   - ☐ **b.** lower interest rates on loans.
   - ☐ **c.** higher interest rates on loans.

3. A person who wants a good credit history should
   - ☐ **a.** save money.
   - ☐ **b.** pay monthly bills on time.
   - ☐ **c.** never buy anything on credit.

4. From the article, you can conclude that a $15,000 loan at 10 percent interest will cost more than a $15,000 loan at
   - ☐ **a.** 5 percent interest.
   - ☐ **b.** 12 percent interest.
   - ☐ **c.** 20 percent interest.

5. You can also conclude that
   - ☐ **a.** interest rates do not often change.
   - ☐ **b.** consumers pay back more for a loan than they borrow.
   - ☐ **c.** consumers usually choose the amount of interest they want to pay.

C. Reading Strategies

1. Recognizing Words in Context

Find the word *examine* in the article. One definition below is closest to the meaning of that word. One definition has the opposite or nearly the opposite meaning. The remaining definition has a meaning that has nothing to do with the word. Label the definitions **C** for *closest*, **O** for *opposite* or *nearly opposite*, and **U** for *unrelated*.

_____ **a.** believe

_____ **b.** ignore

_____ **c.** look at

2. Distinguishing Fact from Opinion

Two of the statements below present *facts*, which can be proved. The other statement is an *opinion*, which expresses someone's thoughts or beliefs. Label the statements **F** for *fact* and **O** for *opinion*.

_____ **a.** Banks borrow money from the Federal Reserve Bank.

_____ **b.** Borrowers may need to improve their credit to get a loan from a bank.

_____ **c.** Borrowers should not get a loan at an interest rate higher than 5 percent.

3. Making Correct Inferences

Two of the statements below are correct *inferences,* or reasonable guesses, that are based on information in the article. The other statement is an incorrect inference. Label the statements **C** for *correct* inference and **I** for *incorrect* inference.

_____ **a.** Banks may lower their interest rates to attract more customers.

_____ **b.** Banks offer the same interest rates to all of their customers.

_____ **c.** Lenders can decide whether or not to give a loan to a borrower.

4. Understanding Main Ideas

One of the statements below expresses the main idea of the article. Another statement is too general, or too broad. The other explains only part of the article; it is too narrow. Label the statements **M** for *main idea,* **B** for *too broad,* and **N** for *too narrow.*

_____ **a.** A borrower must pay interest in exchange for a loan.

_____ **b.** Banks give loans to borrowers for a profit.

_____ **c.** Banks decide whether to loan money to people, and they charge interest on loans.

5. Responding to the Article

Complete the following sentence in your own words:

Reading "The Business of Borrowing Money" made me want to learn more about

_____

because _____

_____

D. Expanding Vocabulary

Content-Area Words

Complete each sentence with a word from the box. Write the missing word on the line.

mortgage	lend	credit	profit	interest

1. Rico was cold, so I offered to _____ him my coat.

2. My father needed to get a _____ loan to buy our new house.

3. Susan decided not to get the loan because of its high _____ rate.

4. If a business keeps its costs low, it can earn a higher _____.

5. If people fail to pay their bills, it is bad for their _____.

Academic English

In the article "The Business of Borrowing Money," you learned that *available* means "ready to have or to use." *Available* can describe interest rates that borrowers can get at different banks. *Available* can also describe other things that are ready to have or to use, as in the following sentence.

Snow shovels are available in stores during the winter.

Complete the sentence below.

1. It was difficult to find an *available* seat at _____

Now use the word *available* in a sentence of your own.

2. _____

_____

You also learned that *factors* means "things that cause results or that are important parts in a situation." *Factors* can also mean "numbers that form a certain product when someone multiplies them together," as in the following sentence.

The numbers 2 and 6 are factors of 12, because 2 × 6 = 12.

Complete the sentence below.

3. Two *factors* of the number 8 are _____

Now use the word *factors* in two sentences of your own.

4. _____

5. _____

 Share your new sentences with a partner.

Reading a Brochure

Read the brochure. Then complete the sentences. Use words from the Word Bank.

Word Bank
budget
available
arrange
selection
final

Learn to Fly!

Discover the thrill of flying a plane at the Lindbergh Flight Center! We have a large (1)_____ of flight classes. Most classes are (2)_____ all year, but some take place only during the summer. You can decide what types of planes you would like to fly, and then we will help you choose which class is best for you.

Are you worried that flying lessons will not fit into your (3)_____? We can (4)_____ payment plans to meet your needs. By the (5)_____ lesson, you will feel comfortable and confident in your own plane. Come and find out what it is like to have wings!

Reading an Interview

Read the interview. Circle the word that completes each sentence.

Daily News • Social Studies

An Interview with Web Snack Shop Owner Isabel Carrido
by Ku Xiong, President of Future Business Owners Club, Hampton Middle School

Ku Xiong: Ms. Carrido, when did you (**host, establish**) your restaurant?

Isabel Carrido: I started this business four years ago. I wanted to open a business that would interest people of all ages.

Ku Xiong: What (**factors, records**) have been important to the success of your business?

Isabel Carrido: To start with, the (**coefficient, design**) for the seating area looks like someone's home. This makes people feel comfortable. Another important

(**event, feature**) is the laptop computers on each table. People can enjoy the Internet while they eat.

Ku Xiong: Tell me about the building in which the restaurant is located.

Isabel Carrido: The building was (**constructed, connected**) in 1900. The decorations are a mix of old and modern styles.

Ku Xiong: Thanks for talking with me, Ms. Carrido. Many Hampton students have told me that they enjoy your Web Snack Shop!

 **Making Connections**

Work with a partner. Talk about what the words mean. List the words from the box in the first column of the chart. In the second column, write a word or phrase that has a meaning that is similar to the meaning of each word. In the third column, write a word or phrase that shows what the first two words make you think of.

theory	compute	ancient	proved	lend
profit	networks	adjustments	numerals	friction

Word	Similar Word	What It Makes Me Think Of

Use all of the words above in complete sentences of your own. Each sentence may include one or more of the words. To help you start writing, look at the ideas you wrote about in the chart. After you write your sentences, read them over. If you find a mistake, correct it.

How Did Our Calendar Develop?

Before You Read

 Think about what you know. Read the lesson title above. Think about what you already know about the calendar we use today. Who do you think invented our calendar?

Vocabulary

The content-area and academic English words below appear in "How Did Our Calendar Develop?" Read the definitions and the example sentences.

Content-Area Words

calendar (kal'ən dər) a way to divide time into set amounts throughout a year
Example: The *calendar* people use in the United States has 12 months in a year.

solar (sō'lər) having to do with the Sun
Example: *Solar* cars use energy from the Sun to move.

leap year (lēp yēr) a calendar year with an extra day that occurs every fourth year
Example: February 29 is the date that only occurs in a *leap year*.

cycle (sī'kəl) a group of events that occur over and over in a certain order
Example: The *cycle* of seasons includes winter, spring, summer, and fall.

lunar (lōō'nər) having to do with the Moon
Example: We see different amounts of the Moon's surface during the *lunar* cycle.

Academic English

created (krē āt'əd) made something; caused something to exist
Example: I *created* a beautiful picture in art class.

method (meth'əd) a way of doing something that helps to reach a goal
Example: Making note cards is one *method* for studying new words.

Do any of the words above seem related? Sort the seven vocabulary words into three categories. Write the words down on note cards or in a chart. Words may fit into more than one group. You may wish to work with a partner for this activity. Label the categories *The Sky*, *Time*, and *Other*.

 Now skim the article and look for other words that are new to you. Write each new word and its definition in the Personal Dictionary.

While You Read

 Think about why you read. How do you use the calendar in your daily life? Do you know the name of the calendar we use? As you read, try to find the answer.

How Did Our Calendar Develop?

1   The type of **calendar** that people use most often is called a *solar calendar*. *Solar* means "having to do with the Sun." The solar calendar is based on how long it takes Earth to travel once around the Sun. Earth makes this journey around the Sun in 365 ¼ days. The calendar has 365 days every three out of four years.
5   It has 366 days every fourth year. The calendar combines the four one-quarter days into one day and adds it to the fourth year. This year is a **leap year.** The extra day in a leap year is February 29.

The solar calendar is not the only way to count the months. People in earlier times used the **cycle** of the Moon to create their calendars. Their months started
10 with the new moon phase, or the part of the cycle when people cannot see the Moon in the sky. The months lasted about 29 days. Calendars that use the cycle of the Moon are called *lunar calendars*. Some people still use lunar calendars today.

The Romans **created** the solar calendar about 2,000 years ago. Before that time, the ancient Romans used a version, or type, of the lunar calendar. This
15 calendar lasted 304 days and had 10 months. This equaled an average of 30.4 days per month. Then the Roman emperor Julius Caesar traveled to Egypt. In Egypt he learned the Egyptian **method** of time measurement. When Caesar returned to Rome, he changed the calendar. He replaced the lunar calendar with a solar calendar that had 12 months. This calendar counted 365 days every three
20 out of four years, with a leap year every fourth year.

In 1582 Pope Gregory XIII, with the help of his scientists, made more changes to the solar calendar. It became the calendar that most people use today. People call this calendar the *Gregorian calendar*. It is similar to Caesar's calendar. It sets the year at 365 days with a leap year every fourth year. The Gregorian calendar
25 worked better than Caesar's calendar and other earlier calendars. However, people did not begin to use it in many places until the twentieth century.

The months of the solar calendar have different numbers of days. It can be difficult to remember how many days are in each month. Many years ago, someone created the following rhyme to help people remember how many days
30 are in each month:

Thirty days have September,
April, June, and November.
All the rest have thirty-one,
Except February the only one
Which leap years change each fourth time
From twenty-eight to twenty-nine.

After You Read

A. Organizing Ideas

What are the differences between solar and lunar calendars? Complete the diagram below. In the left circle, list important facts about solar calendars. In the right circle, list important facts about lunar calendars. Use the article to find information. Some have been done for you.

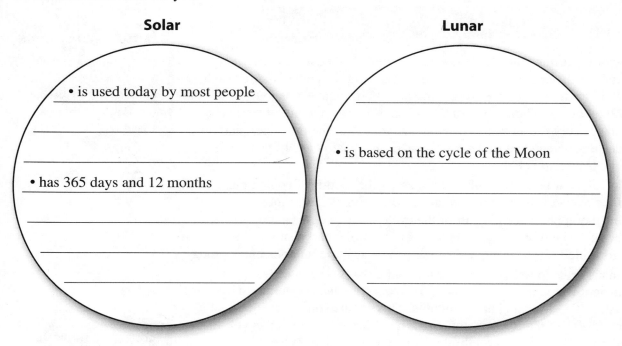

Solar

Lunar

• is used today by most people

_____

_____

• has 365 days and 12 months

_____

_____

_____

_____

• is based on the cycle of the Moon

_____

_____

_____

How have calendars changed from ancient times to today? Why did the calendars change? Write two or more sentences to answer these questions. How did this diagram help you organize information?

_____

_____

_____

_____

_____

_____

B. Comprehension Skills

Tip! **Think about how to find answers.** Look back at different parts of the text. What facts help you figure out how to complete the sentences?

Mark box **a, b,** or **c** with an **X** before the choice that best completes each sentence.

Recalling Facts

1. The calendar most often used today
   - ☐ **a.** has always been the way it is now.
   - ☐ **b.** is based on the cycle of the Moon.
   - ☐ **c.** is similar to Caesar's calendar.

2. The solar calendar people use today is
   - ☐ **a.** the Caesar calendar.
   - ☐ **b.** the February calendar.
   - ☐ **c.** the Gregorian calendar.

3. The solar calendar has leap years because
   - ☐ **a.** the lunar cycle is 28 days.
   - ☐ **b.** Earth takes 365 ¼ days to travel once around the Sun.
   - ☐ **c.** people cannot agree on the number of days in a year.

4. Lunar calendar months last about
   - ☐ **a.** 27 days.
   - ☐ **b.** 29 days.
   - ☐ **c.** 31 days.

5. A year in the Roman lunar calendar had
   - ☐ **a.** 10 months and 304 days.
   - ☐ **b.** 10 months and 365 days.
   - ☐ **c.** 12 months and 304 days.

Understanding Ideas

1. From the article, you can conclude that
   - ☐ **a.** calendars are based on natural cycles.
   - ☐ **b.** the current calendar will never change.
   - ☐ **c.** the lunar calendar was correct more often than the solar calendar was.

2. You can also conclude that the people who developed the lunar calendar were probably
   - ☐ **a.** astronomers who studied the Moon.
   - ☐ **b.** people who did not want Julius Caesar to be the emperor.
   - ☐ **c.** people whose lives and work were closely tied to the lunar cycle.

3. Many people did not use the Gregorian calendar until the twentieth century probably because they
   - ☐ **a.** did not want to change.
   - ☐ **b.** did not like Pope Gregory XIII.
   - ☐ **c.** thought that it was incorrect.

4. The only months with 30 days are
   - ☐ **a.** March, June, and September.
   - ☐ **b.** September, October, and November.
   - ☐ **c.** April, June, September, and November.

5. The solar calendar is probably related to
   - ☐ **a.** the cycle of the Moon.
   - ☐ **b.** the cycle of the seasons.
   - ☐ **c.** both the cycle of the Moon and the cycle of the seasons.

C. Reading Strategies

1. Recognizing Words in Context

Find the word *combines* in the article. One definition below is closest to the meaning of that word. One definition has the opposite or nearly the opposite meaning. The remaining definition has a meaning that has nothing to do with the word. Label the definitions **C** for *closest*, **O** for *opposite* or *nearly opposite*, and **U** for *unrelated*.

_____ **a.** separates

_____ **b.** lifts

_____ **c.** joins

2. Distinguishing Fact from Opinion

Two of the statements below present *facts*, which can be proved. The other statement is an *opinion*, which expresses someone's thoughts or beliefs. Label the statements **F** for *fact* and **O** for *opinion*.

_____ **a.** February has 29 days every fourth year.

_____ **b.** In the calendar most people use today, no months have 32 days.

_____ **c.** The calendar would be easier to understand without leap years.

3. Making Correct Inferences

Two of the statements below are correct *inferences*, or reasonable guesses, that are based on information in the article. The other statement is an incorrect inference. Label the statements **C** for *correct* inference and **I** for *incorrect* inference.

_____ **a.** Caesar thought that the solar calendar was better than the lunar calendar.

_____ **b.** March and August are two months that have 31 days.

_____ **c.** The people who use lunar calendars today do not know about solar calendars.

4. Understanding Main Ideas

One of the statements below expresses the main idea of the article. Another statement is too general, or too broad. The other explains only part of the article; it is too narrow. Label the statements **M** for *main idea*, **B** for *too broad*, and **N** for *too narrow*.

_____ **a.** The shift from lunar to solar calendars was important in our calendar's history.

_____ **b.** Both Julius Caesar and Pope Gregory XIII helped develop the solar calendar.

_____ **c.** Throughout history, people have used calendars to measure time.

5. Responding to the Article

Complete the following sentence in your own words:

Before reading "How Did Our Calendar Develop?" I already knew

_____

_____

D. Expanding Vocabulary

Content-Area Words

Read each item carefully. Write on the line the word or phrase that best completes each sentence.

1. The calendar we use today has 12 months and _____ days.
   365 or 366   366   304

2. A leap year has _____ in February.
   one less day   an extra day   an extra week

3. A solar flashlight uses energy from the light of _____.
   a lightbulb   the Sun   the Moon

4. The appearance of the Moon _____ throughout its cycle.
   changes   becomes smaller   stays the same

5. Lunar calendars are based on _____.
   the stars   the Sun   the Moon

Academic English

In the article "How Did Our Calendar Develop?" you learned that *created* means "made something" or "caused something to exist." *Created* can also mean "produced in the imagination or the thoughts," as in the following sentence.

The author created many exciting characters for her book.

Complete the sentence below.

1. My brother *created* a plan to improve his _____

Now use the word *created* in a sentence of your own.

2. _____

You also learned that *method* means "a way of doing something that helps to reach a goal." *Method* can also mean "order" or "arrangement," as in the following sentence.

Tim took a long time to unload the truck because his system had no method.

Complete the sentence below.

3. Students who have no *method* in their study plans may _____

Now use the word *method* in two sentences of your own.

4. _____

5. _____

 Share your new sentences with a partner.

Before You Read

 Think about what you know. Read the lesson title above. What do you think the article will be about? What do you already know about the pyramids of Egypt?

Vocabulary

The content-area and academic English words below appear in "The Pyramids of Egypt." Read the definitions and the example sentences.

Content-Area Words

pyramid (pir′ə mid′) a structure with a square base and four triangular sides that form a point at the top

    Example: I wonder how the Egyptians built this huge stone *pyramid*.

base (bās) the bottom part that supports something that stands on it

    Example: My family built the house on a *base* of brick and concrete.

margin (mär′jin) amount or degree of difference

    Example: The *margin* between my sister's height and mine is two inches.

tons (tunz) units of weight equal to about 2,000 pounds

    Example: An adult male elephant can weigh as much as seven *tons*.

inclined planes (in klīnd′ plānz) tilted surfaces that people use to move heavy objects

    Example: They used *inclined planes* to roll heavy furniture into the house.

Academic English

site (sīt) the place where something is, was, or will be

    Example: Many machines are at the building *site* for the new library.

achieve (ə chēv′) to get or do something successfully

    Example: Students should try to *achieve* good grades in school.

Read again the example sentences that follow the content-area and academic English word definitions. With a partner, discuss the meanings of the words and sentences.

 Now skim the article and look for other words that are new to you. Write each new word and its definition in the Personal Dictionary.

While You Read

Think about why you read. Have you ever wondered how the Egyptians built the pyramids? As you read, look for information about how the Egyptians moved the giant stones. Think about how builders would do this differently today.

The Pyramids of Egypt

1 The Great **Pyramid** is one of the Seven Wonders of the Ancient World. The Egyptians built the pyramid for the pharaoh Khufu, a leader of the Egyptian people. When he died, they buried him in a room at the center of the pyramid. The stones of the room fitted together so well that a card could not pass between them. 5 The Great Pyramid is more than 4,500 years old. It is the oldest of the Seven Wonders. It is also the only one that still stands.

To build the Great Pyramid, the Egyptians needed to measure a square **base.** The base has four right angles, or angles that measure 90 degrees. The base of the pyramid is level, or even in height, within a **margin** of 2.1 centimeters. This is less 10 than 1 inch. The base covers about 13 acres of land. It is 751 feet long on each side. The four corners of the base point exactly to the north, south, east, and west.

The Egyptians carved more than 2.3 million blocks from stone such as limestone and granite. The Egyptians then pulled, pushed, and dragged the blocks for miles to the building **site.** The average weight of each block was about 2.5 **tons,** or about 15 5,000 pounds. Some of the blocks weighed as much as 16 tons, or 32,000 pounds. The Egyptians needed about 20 years to complete the Great Pyramid.

A major problem for the builders of the Great Pyramid was how to get the large stone blocks into place. Most people agree on the method the Egyptians used to **achieve** this. Most people think that the Egyptians built ramps on **inclined planes** 20 made of brick and rocks. They made the ramps slick, or slippery, with water and mud. The workers then pushed and dragged the blocks up the slippery ramps. As the pyramid grew taller, the ramps had to be longer. The inclined planes that supported the ramps also had to be longer. The Egyptians also had to make the bases of the inclined planes wider. Otherwise they would have collapsed under 25 the great weight.

The Great Pyramid is 481 feet high. The Egyptians had no tools to measure the height of the pyramid. The Greek mathematician Thales visited Egypt. He showed the Egyptians how to measure the height of a pyramid. He waited for the time of day when the length of his shadow equaled his own height. From his knowledge 30 of mathematics, Thales knew that at this same moment, the length of the pyramid's shadow must equal the height of the pyramid. Thales simply measured the shadow of the pyramid.

CONTENT CONNECTION

Have you ever heard of the Seven Wonders of the Ancient World? They are the seven most amazing things that people built in the ancient world. Why do you think the Great Pyramid is one of the Seven Wonders?

LANGUAGE CONNECTION

The word *this* is used in line 19 as a pronoun. It refers to an idea that the article has already talked about. Can you describe what *this* refers to? Hint: Reread the first two sentences of the paragraph.

After You Read

A. Organizing Ideas

How did the Egyptians build the pyramids? Complete the chart below. In the left column, write down problems that the Egyptians needed to solve as they built the pyramids. In the right column, write down how they solved the problems. Use the article to help you. Some have been done for you.

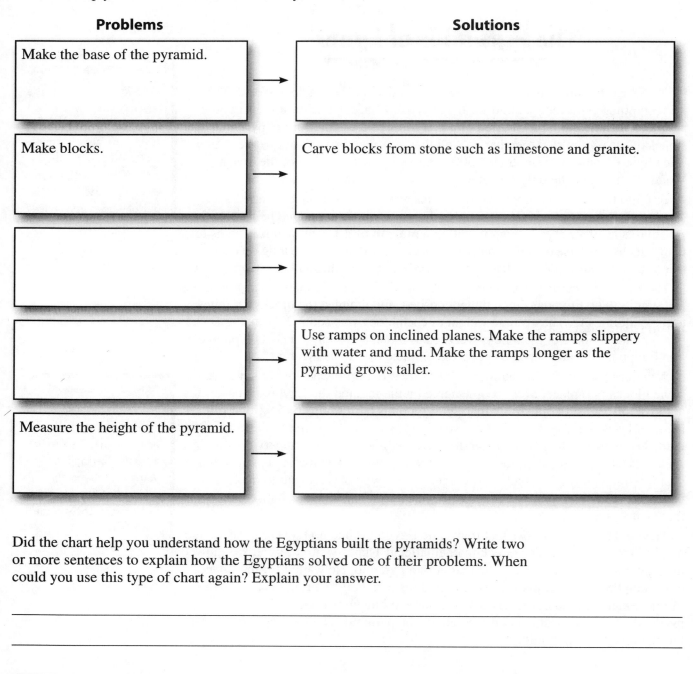

Problems		Solutions
Make the base of the pyramid.	→	
Make blocks.	→	Carve blocks from stone such as limestone and granite.
	→	
	→	Use ramps on inclined planes. Make the ramps slippery with water and mud. Make the ramps longer as the pyramid grows taller.
Measure the height of the pyramid.	→	

Did the chart help you understand how the Egyptians built the pyramids? Write two or more sentences to explain how the Egyptians solved one of their problems. When could you use this type of chart again? Explain your answer.

_____

_____

_____

B. Comprehension Skills

 Think about how to find answers. Look back at what you read. The words in an answer are usually contained in a single sentence.

Mark box **a, b,** or **c** with an **X** before the choice that best completes each sentence.

Recalling Facts

1. The Great Pyramid is
   - ☐ **a.** the tallest structure in the world.
   - ☐ **b.** a temple for an Egyptian pharaoh.
   - ☐ **c.** where the Egyptians buried the pharaoh Khufu.

2. People built the Great Pyramid about
   - ☐ **a.** 400 years ago.
   - ☐ **b.** 4,500 years ago.
   - ☐ **c.** 40,000 years ago.

3. The pyramid's square base is level within a margin of
   - ☐ **a.** 2.1 inches.
   - ☐ **b.** less than 1 inch.
   - ☐ **c.** 1.2 centimeters.

4. The Egyptians moved the stone blocks into place with a system of
   - ☐ **a.** ropes and sleds.
   - ☐ **b.** carts and levers.
   - ☐ **c.** ramps and inclined planes.

5. Thales knew the height of the pyramid because
   - ☐ **a.** it was longer than the length of his own shadow.
   - ☐ **b.** it was the same as the length of the pyramid's shadow.
   - ☐ **c.** the shadow of an object is always longer than the object.

Understanding Ideas

1. The Egyptians probably
   - ☐ **a.** knew the weight of each stone.
   - ☐ **b.** improved their building methods over many years.
   - ☐ **c.** found the four right angles of the square base by accident.

2. The ramps and the inclined planes were longest
   - ☐ **a.** in the late stages of building.
   - ☐ **b.** in the early stages of building.
   - ☐ **c.** in the middle stages of building.

3. The inclined planes
   - ☐ **a.** were shorter than the ramps.
   - ☐ **b.** made it harder to slide the stones up the ramps.
   - ☐ **c.** held up the ramps under the weight of the stones.

4. From the article, you can conclude that a square
   - ☐ **a.** has four equal sides.
   - ☐ **b.** is level to within an inch.
   - ☐ **c.** points exactly to the north, south, east, and west.

5. You can also conclude that the height of a pyramid is the distance
   - ☐ **a.** around the base.
   - ☐ **b.** from the top of the pyramid to the center of the base.
   - ☐ **c.** from one corner to the opposite corner.

C. Reading Strategies

1. Recognizing Words in Context

Find the word *collapsed* in the article. One definition below is closest to the meaning of that word. One definition has the opposite or nearly the opposite meaning. The remaining definition has a meaning that has nothing to do with the word. Label the definitions **C** for *closest*, **O** for *opposite* or *nearly opposite*, and **U** for *unrelated*.

_____ **a.** stayed up

_____ **b.** fallen

_____ **c.** become larger

2. Distinguishing Fact from Opinion

Two of the statements below present *facts*, which can be proved. The other statement is an *opinion*, which expresses someone's thoughts or beliefs. Label the statements **F** for *fact* and **O** for *opinion*.

_____ **a.** The Great Pyramid still stands in Egypt.

_____ **b.** The easiest way to measure the height of something is to measure its shadow.

_____ **c.** The Egyptians probably used inclined planes to build the Great Pyramid.

3. Making Correct Inferences

Two of the statements below are correct *inferences*, or reasonable guesses, that are based on information in the article. The other statement is an incorrect inference. Label the statements **C** for *correct* inference and **I** for *incorrect* inference.

_____ **a.** Thales stayed in Egypt for many years.

_____ **b.** Many workers helped build the Great Pyramid.

_____ **c.** The Egyptians built the pyramids to honor important people.

4. Understanding Main Ideas

One of the statements below expresses the main idea of the article. Another statement is too general, or too broad. The other explains only part of the article; it is too narrow. Label the statements **M** for *main idea*, **B** for *too broad*, and **N** for *too narrow*.

_____ **a.** It took about 20 years for the Egyptians to build the Great Pyramid.

_____ **b.** The Great Pyramid still stands, even though the Egyptians used simple tools to build it.

_____ **c.** The Great Pyramid is one of the Seven Wonders of the Ancient World.

5. Responding to the Article

Complete the following sentence in your own words:

What interested me most in "The Pyramids of Egypt" was

_____

_____

D. Expanding Vocabulary

Content-Area Words

Cross out one word in each row that is not related to the word in dark type.

1. pyramid	Egypt	wood	stone	triangles
2. base	bottom	support	lowest	top
3. margin	sharp	amount	difference	measure
4. tons	weight	heavy	measurement	taste
5. inclined planes	ramp	light	surface	angle

Academic English

In the article "The Pyramids of Egypt," you learned that *site* means "the place where something is, was, or will be." *Site* can also mean "the position of a place in relation to the area or region around it," as in the following sentence.

The mountain site of the town made it difficult to drive there.

Complete the sentence below.

1. The camp had a forest *site,* so it had a lot of _____

Now use the word *site* in a sentence of your own.

2. _____

_____

You also learned that *achieve* means "to get or do something successfully."
Achieve can also mean "to be successful," as in the following sentence.

The dance teacher wanted all of his students to achieve.

Complete the sentence below.

3. If you want to *achieve* in sports, you must _____

Now use the word *achieve* in two sentences of your own.

4. _____

5. _____

 Share your new sentences with a partner.

Before You Read

 Think about what you know. Read the lesson title above. What do you think the article will be about? Do you know how to measure a circle?

Vocabulary

The content-area and academic English words below appear in "Measuring Circles." Read the definitions and the example sentences.

Content-Area Words

geometry (jē om′ə trē) the area of mathematics that studies points, lines, and shapes
> *Example:* In *geometry* students learn how to measure shapes, such as squares.

radius (rā′dē əs) the distance from the center of a circle to a point on the circumference
> *Example:* The *radius* of a music CD is between two and three inches.

circumference (sər kum′fər əns) the distance around a circle
> *Example:* The distance around a round dinner plate is its *circumference*.

diameter (dī am′ə tər) a straight line that begins at any point on a circle, passes through the center of the circle, and ends on the opposite side of the circle
> *Example:* The *diameter* of the large pizza was 16 inches.

compass (kum′pəs) an instrument that people use to draw perfect circles
> *Example:* I use a *compass* to draw circles in math class.

Academic English

derived (di rīvd′) traced back to a certain source or starting point
> *Example:* Many English words are *derived* from Latin or Greek words.

principle (prin′sə pəl) a rule that explains how something works
> *Example:* The *principle* of gravity explains why an apple falls from a tree.

Rate each vocabulary word according to the following scale. Write a number next to each content-area and academic English word.

4   I have never seen the word before.

3   I have seen the word but do not know what it means.

2   I know what the word means when I read it.

1   I use the word myself in speaking or writing.

 Now skim the article and look for other words that are new to you. Write each new word and its definition in the Personal Dictionary.

While You Read

 Think about why you read. Do you think it is useful to know how to measure a circle? As you read, look for the way that you can use the circumference of a circle to figure out how far you have traveled in a car.

Measuring Circles

1 **G**eometry is the type of mathematics that studies points, lines, planes, and shapes, including circles. Examples of circles are everywhere.

All points on a circle are the same distance from the center of the circle. In other words, a true circle is perfectly round. A person can draw a straight line 5 from the center of a circle to any point on the circle. The distance from the center to that point is the **radius.**

The distance around a circle is the **circumference.** The word *circumference* is **derived** from the Latin word *circum,* which means "around." A circle contains 360 degrees. A semicircle is half of a circle, so it contains 180 degrees. The 10 **diameter** of a circle is a straight line that can start from any point on the circle. It goes through the center and ends on the exact opposite side of the circle. This means that a diameter equals the length of two radii. If two or more diameters start from different points on a circle, they form angles. For example, when you slice a round pizza, you usually slice along several diameters. If you slice a pizza 15 into eight equal pieces, each piece will have a 45-degree angle.

People can use circles to measure other things. Imagine that you are riding your bike. Each time a bike wheel rolls around once, it travels a distance equal to the circumference of the wheel. If you know the circumference of the wheel, then you know how far you have traveled. The same **principle** works in a car. The 20 mileage counter in a car counts the number of times the car wheels roll around.

A **compass** is an instrument that people use to draw circles. This kind of compass is different from the compass that shows direction. It has two legs connected by a pivot, which is a joint that holds the legs together. The pivot can also change the angle between the legs. One leg has a pointed end that holds the 25 compass in place on a piece of paper. The other leg holds a pencil. As someone turns the compass, the pencil traces a circle.

The distance around a circle is about three times the length of the diameter. This is true for all circles. When people divide the circumference by the diameter, they get a number that is approximately 3.14. This is the value people use for the 30 number called *pi,* or π. Nobody can write down the full value for pi, because it goes on forever to the right of the decimal point. Pi is the same number for every circle.

LANGUAGE CONNECTION

What is the plural of the word *radius?* In other words, how would you say "more than one radius"? Continue to read to see if you are correct.

CONTENT CONNECTION

The distance between the pointed end of a compass and the tip of the pencil is equal to the radius of the circle it draws. If this distance is four inches, how long is the diameter?

After You Read

A. Applying the Math

What are the different parts of a circle? Label the parts of the circle below. Use all of the words in the box. You will need to draw some of the parts before you label them. Refer to the article for help. Some have been done for you.

where the point of a compass goes		
radius	diameter	circumference
90°	180°	360°

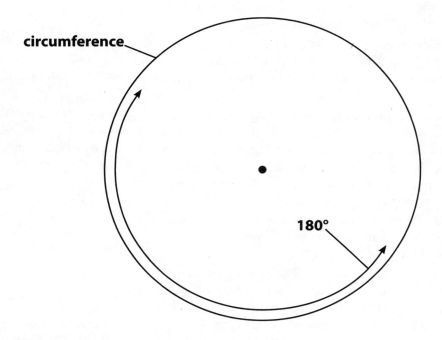

circumference

180°

Did labeling the parts of the circle help you understand the information you read? Why or why not? Write two or more sentences to answer these questions. Do you think that labeling parts could also help you understand other shapes? Explain your answer.

_____

_____

_____

_____

B. Comprehension Skills

 Think about how to find answers. Look back at what you read. The information is in the text, but you may have to look in several sentences to find it.

Mark box **a, b,** or **c** with an **X** before the choice that best completes each sentence.

Recalling Facts

1. The distance around a circle is
- ☐ **a.** pi.
- ☐ **b.** the diameter.
- ☐ **c.** the circumference.

2. The word *circumference* is derived from a Latin word that means
- ☐ **a.** "around."
- ☐ **b.** "through."
- ☐ **c.** "perimeter."

3. It is not true that
- ☐ **a.** a circle contains 360 degrees.
- ☐ **b.** the diameter is the distance around a circle.
- ☐ **c.** the distance around a circle is about three times the distance across the circle.

4. The distance from the center of a circle to any point on the circle is
- ☐ **a.** the radius.
- ☐ **b.** the diameter.
- ☐ **c.** the circumference.

5. The distance around a circle is about three times
- ☐ **a.** pi.
- ☐ **b.** the radius.
- ☐ **c.** the distance across the circle.

Understanding Ideas

1. Someone can use a compass to
- ☐ **a.** draw a perfect circle.
- ☐ **b.** find the radius of a circle.
- ☐ **c.** find the diameter of a circle.

2. If someone cuts a round pizza into four equal pieces, each piece will have an angle of
- ☐ **a.** 45 degrees.
- ☐ **b.** 90 degrees.
- ☐ **c.** 180 degrees.

3. The radius of a circle
- ☐ **a.** is half of the diameter.
- ☐ **b.** divides the circle in half.
- ☐ **c.** is the distance around the circle.

4. The number of diameters that creates four 90-degree angles is
- ☐ **a.** two.
- ☐ **b.** four.
- ☐ **c.** six.

5. When a person who is facing north turns to face south, that person turns
- ☐ **a.** 90 degrees.
- ☐ **b.** 180 degrees.
- ☐ **c.** 360 degrees.

C. Reading Strategies

1. Recognizing Words in Context

Find the word *approximately* in the article. One definition below is closest to the meaning of that word. One definition has the opposite or nearly the opposite meaning. The remaining definition has a meaning that has nothing to do with the word. Label the definitions **C** for *closest,* **O** for *opposite* or *nearly opposite,* and **U** for *unrelated.*

_____ **a.** happily

_____ **b.** exactly

_____ **c.** about

2. Distinguishing Fact from Opinion

Two of the statements below present *facts,* which can be proved. The other statement is an *opinion,* which expresses someone's thoughts or beliefs. Label the statements **F** for *fact* and **O** for *opinion.*

_____ **a.** People usually use 3.14 as the value of pi.

_____ **b.** The diameter of a circle must pass through the center of the circle.

_____ **c.** Geometry is a difficult area of mathematics.

3. Making Correct Inferences

Two of the statements below are correct *inferences,* or reasonable guesses, that are based on information in the article. The other statement is an incorrect inference. Label the statements **C** for *correct* inference and **I** for *incorrect* inference.

_____ **a.** Any line that connects one point on a circle to another is a diameter.

_____ **b.** To find the radius, divide the length of a diameter by 2.

_____ **c.** A basketball has a larger circumference than a baseball does.

4. Understanding Main Ideas

One of the statements below expresses the main idea of the article. Another statement is too general, or too broad. The other explains only part of the article; it is too narrow. Label the statements **M** for *main idea,* **B** for *too broad,* and **N** for *too narrow.*

_____ **a.** Circles are round shapes that people study in geometry.

_____ **b.** People can measure circles by their circumference, radius, and diameter.

_____ **c.** A perfect circle drawn with a compass contains 360 degrees.

5. Responding to the Article

Complete the following sentence in your own words:

From reading "Measuring Circles," I have learned

_____

_____

D. Expanding Vocabulary

Content-Area Words

Read each item carefully. Write on the line the word or phrase that best completes each sentence.

1. She uses a compass to _____ in math class.
    measure circles   draw circles   make circles larger

2. Measure the _____ a circle to find its circumference.
    distance around   space inside   number of degrees in

3. If I study geometry in school, I may learn about _____.
    shapes   paragraphs   chemicals

4. The diameter is a line that goes _____ a circle.
    under   around   through

5. The radius of a pizza probably would be closest to _____.
    one inch   six inches   thirty inches

Academic English

In the article "Measuring Circles," you learned that *derived* means "traced back to a certain source or starting point." *Derived* can also mean "got something from another source or substance," as in the following sentence.

    Both sugar and chocolate are derived from plants.

Complete the sentence below.

1. Peanut butter is *derived* from _____

Now use the word *derived* in a sentence of your own.

2. _____

You also learned that *principle* means "a rule that explains how something works." *Principle* can also mean "a rule about how someone should behave," as in the following sentence.

    Honesty, or telling the truth, is a principle that is important to me.

Complete the sentence below.

3. Tony's mother taught him the *principle* that it is not right to cheat on _____

Now use the word *principle* in two sentences of your own.

4. _____

5. _____

 Share your new sentences with a partner.

Before You Read

 Think about what you know. Skim the article on the opposite page. What do you already know about distances in outer space? Are objects in outer space close to each other or far apart?

Vocabulary

The content-area and academic English words below appear in "Distances and Light-Years in Space." Read the definitions and the example sentences.

Content-Area Words

astronomy (əs tron′ə mē) the science of outer space
Example: We learned about the Moon when we studied *astronomy.*

universe (ū′nə vurs′) everything that exists in space, including the stars and the planets
Example: Our solar system is just one small part of the *universe.*

astronomical (as′trə nom′i kəl) extremely large
Example: The Rocky Mountains of the United States are *astronomical* in size.

light-year (līt yēr) the distance that light travels through space in one year
Example: The *light-year* helps scientists measure large distances in outer space.

galaxy (gal′ək sē) a group of stars and clouds of gases and dust
Example: Our *galaxy* includes the Sun as well as billions of other stars.

Academic English

minor (mī′nər) small in size or amount
Example: The accident caused only a *minor* cut on my arm.

consists (kən sists′) is made up of different parts or items
Example: My class *consists* of 10 boys and 13 girls.

Do any of the words above seem related? Sort the seven vocabulary words into three categories. Write the words down on note cards or in a chart. Words may fit into more than one group. You may wish to work with a partner for this activity. Label the categories *Outer Space, Measurements and Sizes,* and *Other.*

 Now skim the article and look for other words that are new to you. Write each new word and its definition in the Personal Dictionary.

While You Read

 Think about why you read. What do you want to learn about outer space? Before you read, turn to the next page. Fill in the first two columns of the chart with facts that you know and questions that you have about distances in outer space. As you read, look for answers to your questions.

DISTANCES AND LIGHT-YEARS IN SPACE

1   **A**stronomy is the science of outer space. Astronomers are people who study the **universe,** which includes all of the stars and the planets. The universe also includes Earth's solar system, which is the Sun and everything that circles around it. Astronomers try to understand how large the universe is and how many
5   years it has existed. Astronomers do not measure distances in outer space the way people measure distances on Earth. For example, have you ever heard someone say that something is **"astronomical"?** If you want to say that something is really big, such as a distance in space, you can use the word *astronomical*.

Earth's sun is a star. It is the closest star to Earth. The Sun is about 93 million
10 miles away. The next closest star after the Sun is about 24 trillion miles away! Light from the Sun has to travel a great distance to reach Earth. Light travels quickly, at about 186,282 miles per second. The speed of light is always the same.

Scientists use the term *light-year* to refer to how far light travels in one Earth year. Astronomers use light-years to measure the huge distances in outer space.

15 A light-year equals a certain number of actual miles. To find this number, first calculate the number of seconds in a year: 60 seconds $\times$ 60 minutes $\times$ 24 hours $\times$ 365.25 days in a year $=$ 31,557,600 seconds. Then multiply the number of seconds in a year by the speed of light (186,282 miles per second). One light-year is about 5,878,612,843,200 miles. This means that in one year, light can travel
20 almost 6 trillion miles through space. This great distance, however, is still only about one fourth of the distance to the star that is closest to Earth's sun. Compared to the size of the entire universe, a single light-year is a **minor** distance.

Many astronomers believe that the universe began with a big explosion, or blast, that people call the *Big Bang*. They believe that the Big Bang created all
25 of the materials that later became planets and stars. Astronomers think that the universe is now about 11.2 billion years old. Light that reaches Earth from the farthest known **galaxy** has been traveling for more than 20 billion years.

Earth is part of the Milky Way galaxy. The Milky Way **consists** of the Sun, the nine known planets that orbit it, and billions of other stars. Look at the stars one
30 night. Some starlight may have started out from stars billions of years ago.

LANGUAGE CONNECTION

Look at the words *astronomy, astronomers,* and *astronomical.* Which of them is the root word of all three words? What does the root word mean?

CONTENT CONNECTION

One light-year equals about 6 trillion miles. Other than the Sun, the closest star to Earth is 24 trillion miles away. How long does it take for light from that star to reach Earth?

After You Read

A. Organizing Ideas

What do you know or want to know about distances in outer space? Complete the chart below. List four facts that you already know about distances in space and four things that you want to learn about. After you read the article, list four facts that you learned from the article.

Distances in Space

What I Know	What I Want to Know	What I Have Learned

Did this chart help you learn more about something that you already knew? Write two or more sentences about what you knew about distances in space before you read the article and what you know now. Would you use this type of chart again? Why or why not?

_____

_____

_____

B. Comprehension Skills

 Think about how to find answers. Think about what each sentence means. Try to say it to yourself in your own words before you complete it.

Mark box **a, b,** or **c** with an **X** before the choice that best completes each sentence.

Recalling Facts

1. Astronomers study
   - ☐ **a.** Earth.
   - ☐ **b.** the universe.
   - ☐ **c.** the effects of stars on people.

2. A light-year is
   - ☐ **a.** an amount of time.
   - ☐ **b.** equal to 6 million miles.
   - ☐ **c.** a unit that measures distance.

3. The speed of light is about
   - ☐ **a.** 186,000 miles per second.
   - ☐ **b.** 6 billion miles per second.
   - ☐ **c.** 24 trillion miles per second.

4. Many astronomers believe that an event called the Big Bang
   - ☐ **a.** destroyed millions of planets.
   - ☐ **b.** occurred 37 billion years ago.
   - ☐ **c.** created the material that formed the universe.

5. The Milky Way is
   - ☐ **a.** a planet.
   - ☐ **b.** a galaxy.
   - ☐ **c.** a solar system.

Understanding Ideas

1. The light of the Sun travels to the planet Mars and to Earth
   - ☐ **a.** at 1 mile per hour.
   - ☐ **b.** at the same speed.
   - ☐ **c.** at different speeds.

2. An astronomer would say that light-years
   - ☐ **a.** are smaller than miles in space.
   - ☐ **b.** are units that measure starlight.
   - ☐ **c.** are easier to use than miles for measuring distances in space.

3. Light from the Sun reaches Earth in less than one light-year because
   - ☐ **a.** the Sun is in the same galaxy as Earth.
   - ☐ **b.** the Sun is less than 6 trillion miles from Earth.
   - ☐ **c.** people use miles instead of light-years to measure the distance between Earth and the Sun.

4. The main idea of the Big Bang is that the universe formed when
   - ☐ **a.** materials from a large explosion became planets and stars.
   - ☐ **b.** materials from planets and stars exploded.
   - ☐ **c.** a large explosion took place.

5. From the article, you can conclude that
   - ☐ **a.** the planets will someday be stars.
   - ☐ **b.** time travels more slowly in space.
   - ☐ **c.** light from some stars may take billions of years to reach Earth.

C. Reading Strategies

1. Recognizing Words in Context

Find the word *existed* in the article. One definition below is closest to the meaning of that word. One definition has the opposite or nearly the opposite meaning. The remaining definition has a meaning that has nothing to do with the word. Label the definitions **C** for *closest*, **O** for *opposite* or *nearly opposite*, and **U** for *unrelated*.

_____ **a.** been real

_____ **b.** been warm

_____ **c.** been gone

2. Distinguishing Fact from Opinion

Two of the statements below present *facts*, which can be proved. The other statement is an *opinion*, which expresses someone's thoughts or beliefs. Label the statements **F** for *fact* and **O** for *opinion*.

_____ **a.** The speed of light is always 186,282 miles per second.

_____ **b.** Scientists should know more about the Milky Way.

_____ **c.** Astronomers think that the universe is 11.2 billion years old.

3. Making Correct Inferences

Two of the statements below are correct *inferences*, or reasonable guesses, that are based on information in the article. The other statement is an incorrect inference. Label the statements **C** for *correct* inference and **I** for *incorrect* inference.

_____ **a.** Astronomers are not yet able to prove many theories about outer space.

_____ **b.** Scientists probably would not use inches to measure distances in outer space.

_____ **c.** The lights in the sky at night all come from things in Earth's solar system.

4. Understanding Main Ideas

One of the statements below expresses the main idea of the article. Another statement is too general, or too broad. The other explains only part of the article; it is too narrow. Label the statements **M** for *main idea*, **B** for *too broad*, and **N** for *too narrow*.

_____ **a.** Because the universe is so big, astronomers have special ways to study it.

_____ **b.** A light-year is a short distance compared to the huge size of the universe.

_____ **c.** Astronomers measure the large distances in space with light-years.

5. Responding to the Article

Complete the following sentence in your own words:

One thing in "Distances and Light-Years in Space" that I cannot understand is

_____

_____

D. Expanding Vocabulary

Content-Area Words

Complete each sentence with a word from the box. Write the missing word on the line.

astronomy	universe	astronomical	light-year	galaxy

1. I did not have enough money to pay the _____ bill at the fancy restaurant.

2. A class about _____ would be a good place to study stars.

3. Everything in space is part of the _____.

4. Earth is part of the Milky Way _____.

5. Astronomers measure distances in space with a unit called a _____.

Academic English

In the article "Distances and Light-Years in Space," you learned that *minor* means "small in size or amount." *Minor* can also mean "not very important," as in the following sentence.

A cold is usually a minor sickness.

Complete the sentence below.

1. I was glad that the accident caused only *minor* damage to my _____

Now use the word *minor* in a sentence of your own.

2. _____

_____

You also learned that *consists* means "is made up of different parts or items." *Consists* can describe galaxies that are made up of different parts. *Consists* can also describe other things that are made up of different parts, as in the following sentence.

My sandwich consists of bread, tomatoes, and cheese.

Complete the sentence below.

3. The United States *consists* of 50 _____

Now use the word *consists* in two sentences of your own.

4. _____

5. _____

 Share your new sentences with a partner.

Before You Read

Tip! **Think about what you know.** Read the lesson title above. What do you think the article will be about? Have you ever heard of accountants?

Vocabulary

The content-area and academic English words below appear in "What Do Business Accountants Do?" Read the definitions and the example sentences.

Content-Area Words

accountants (ə kount′ənts) people who gather and organize information about money
  Example: Accountants help companies manage money.

asset (as′et) money that someone has, or something that is worth money
  Example: A house is an important *asset* because it is worth a lot of money.

liability (lī′ə bil′ə tē) money that someone must pay to a person or company
  Example: The rent that Shohei pays each month is a *liability*.

debit (deb′it) an amount of money that has been spent
  Example: Maria's bank records show a *debit* for groceries.

auditors (ô′də tərz) accountants who make sure that financial statements are correct
  Example: A company must keep good records to give to *auditors*.

Academic English

financial (fi nan′shəl) relating to money and other resources
  Example: When a company buys a building, it makes a *financial* decision.

specific (spi sif′ik) certain; particular
  Example: Lucas's guitar lessons begin at a *specific* time each week.

Answer the questions below about the content-area and academic English words. Write your answers in the spaces provided. The first one has been done for you.

1. What word goes with *a payment on a car?* _____liability_____

2. What word goes with *people who keep records about money?* _____

3. What word goes with *money spent on a shirt?* _____

4. What word goes with *a particular item?* _____

5. What word goes with *people who check financial records?* _____

6. What word goes with *a car that someone owns?* _____

7. What word goes with *anything related to money?* _____

Dictionary Now skim the article and look for other words that are new to you. Write each new word and its definition in the Personal Dictionary.

While You Read

 Think about why you read. Would you want to be an accountant someday? As you read, think about the skills that an accountant needs to have in order to do a good job.

What Do Business Accountants Do?

1   Business **accountants** gather and organize **financial** information for people who own companies. This information helps owners understand the finances, or money and resources, of their companies. In a way, accountants record the histories of companies by writing down the dollar amounts that they receive and pay out.

5   Business accountants list all of the money a company makes or loses on a form called a *general ledger*. This form shows **asset** accounts and **liability** accounts. Assets are money that the company makes or materials that are worth money. Liabilities are money that the company owes to some person or to another company.

   Some costs appear on both sides of the ledger. Others appear on only one side.
10 If the company buys a machine for $100 in cash, the machine would appear on only the assets side. The accountant would add the value of the machine, $100, to the equipment assets of the company. The accountant would also subtract the same amount from the cash assets of the company. The net, or final, change in total assets would be zero. However, if the company bought the machine on credit,
15 the company would have to make payments on it. This machine would then appear on both sides of the ledger. The equipment assets would go up by $100, but the liabilities would also go up by $100.

   An accountant records every change in the company's money as both a **debit** item and a credit item. People call these debits and credits *entries* because the
20 accountant enters them into the general ledger. A credit entry may be money that is available to spend. A debit entry shows money that the company has spent. The name for this system of accounting is *double-entry accounting*.

   The most common job of accountants is to keep financial records. However, many accountants work in **specific** areas. Some large companies hire accountants
25 to design computer programs. The computer programs help the companies keep records. Many accountants work to create better budgets for companies. Others may look for ways to make the profits of the company higher. Tax accountants prepare tax returns, which are forms that show how much tax money a company owes. Tax accountants may also help company leaders understand how new business deals
30 would affect taxes. They must know a great deal about laws that relate to taxes.

   Some accountants work as **auditors.** These people study financial statements, or information that a company tells people about the company's money. Auditors make sure that the financial statements are complete and correct. Auditors who work inside a company make sure that the company is following its accounting
35 plan. Auditors who work outside the company make sure that the company follows the rules of accounting. Accountants have a lot of responsibility, and they must study and train until they know enough to succeed in a job. They must pass a difficult test before they can get a license.

LANGUAGE CONNECTION

The phrase *pay out* is an idiom that means "to pay money to different people." An idiom is a group of words with a special meaning. *Take up* and *take in* are also idioms. If you want to learn to play soccer, do you take up soccer or take in soccer?

CONTENT CONNECTION

Have you heard of debit cards and credit cards? A debit card takes money out of your bank account when you buy something. A credit card lets you spend more money than you have in your account, but you have to pay it back someday. Which card would you rather have? Why?

After You Read

A. Applying the Math

How do general ledgers help businesses understand their money? Imagine that you are the accountant for Armando's Restaurant. Armando gives you a list of the amounts of money he earns and spends each day. Complete the general ledger below. Use all of the items in the box. Then add the amounts to find the total assets and total liabilities. Some have been done for you.

rent: $200	money to pay waiters: $400
cost of food: $1,000	money from customers: $2,400
loan payments: $20	money to pay cooks: $600
money from people who post ads in the restaurant: $100	taxes: $20

General Ledger for Armando's Restaurant

Assets	Asset Amount	Liabilities	Liability Amount
money from customers	$2,400	loan payments	$20
Total Daily Assets:		**Total Daily Liabilites:**	

Armando wants to hire a famous chef for $200 per day. Do you think this would be a good financial decision? Why or why not? Did the general ledger help you answer the question? Explain your answer.

_____

_____

_____

B. Comprehension Skills

Tip! **Think about how to find answers.** Read each sentence below. Underline the words that will help you figure out how to complete each item.

Mark box **a, b,** or **c** with an **X** before the choice that best completes each sentence.

Recalling Facts

1. An accountant records changes to a company's money as
   - ☐ **a.** credits.
   - ☐ **b.** debits.
   - ☐ **c.** both credits and debits.

2. Liability is
   - ☐ **a.** a credit.
   - ☐ **b.** money a company owes.
   - ☐ **c.** money a company has made.

3. The assets of a company
   - ☐ **a.** are its costs.
   - ☐ **b.** are always cash.
   - ☐ **c.** may be materials that are worth money.

4. One job of an auditor is to
   - ☐ **a.** create better budgets for companies.
   - ☐ **b.** design computer programs for companies.
   - ☐ **c.** make sure that financial statements are correct.

5. It is not true that
   - ☐ **a.** accountants must have a license.
   - ☐ **b.** a ledger is a change to a company's money.
   - ☐ **c.** tax accountants must know the laws that relate to taxes.

Understanding Ideas

1. From the article, you can conclude that
   - ☐ **a.** accounting is an important part of every business.
   - ☐ **b.** different accountants keep records in different ways.
   - ☐ **c.** accounting is more important for large businesses than for small ones.

2. If a company bought a cash register for $2,500 on credit,
   - ☐ **a.** its assets would go down by $2,500.
   - ☐ **b.** its liabilities would go down by $2,500.
   - ☐ **c.** both its assets and its liabilities would go up by $2,500.

3. A tax accountant
   - ☐ **a.** writes tax laws for a company.
   - ☐ **b.** decides if a company pays taxes.
   - ☐ **c.** makes sure that a company does not break any tax laws.

4. It is not the job of an accountant to
   - ☐ **a.** buy new equipment.
   - ☐ **b.** suggest ways to save money.
   - ☐ **c.** keep track of how much the company pays its workers.

5. If a company loses money, an accountant probably would first
   - ☐ **a.** look for the cause in the general ledger.
   - ☐ **b.** design a program to keep better records.
   - ☐ **c.** think of ways the company can spend less.

C. Reading Strategies

1. Recognizing Words in Context

Find the word *responsibility* in the article. One definition below is closest to the meaning of that word. One definition has the opposite or nearly the opposite meaning. The remaining definition has a meaning that has nothing to do with the word. Label the definitions **C** for *closest*, **O** for *opposite* or *nearly opposite*, and **U** for *unrelated*.

_____ **a.** important work

_____ **b.** boring work

_____ **c.** work that is not needed

2. Distinguishing Fact from Opinion

Two of the statements below present *facts*, which can be proved. The other statement is an *opinion*, which expresses someone's thoughts or beliefs. Label the statements **F** for *fact* and **O** for *opinion*.

_____ **a.** The job of an accountant is the most important job in a company.

_____ **b.** A general ledger is a record of the assets and liabilities of a company.

_____ **c.** A purchase may be both an asset and a liability.

3. Making Correct Inferences

Two of the statements below are correct *inferences*, or reasonable guesses, that are based on information in the article. The other statement is an incorrect inference. Label the statements **C** for *correct* inference and **I** for *incorrect* inference.

_____ **a.** Accountants make the decisions about how a company spends money.

_____ **b.** Accountants must have math skills to do their jobs.

_____ **c.** Business owners may consult accountants before they make financial decisions.

4. Understanding Main Ideas

One of the statements below expresses the main idea of the article. Another statement is too general, or too broad. The other explains only part of the article; it is too narrow. Label the statements **M** for *main idea*, **B** for *too broad*, and **N** for *too narrow*.

_____ **a.** An accountant records assets and liabilities on the general ledger.

_____ **b.** Accountants know a great deal about money.

_____ **c.** Accountants do many jobs to help companies manage money.

5. Responding to the Article

Complete the following sentence in your own words:

Before reading "What Do Business Accountants Do?" I already knew

_____

_____

D. Expanding Vocabulary

Content-Area Words

Cross out one word in each row that is not related to the word in dark type.

1. **accountants**	taxes	ledger	music	budget
2. **asset**	cash	own	empty	worth
3. **liability**	truth	owe	money	pay
4. **debit**	money	spent	pay	glass
5. **auditors**	accountants	weather	finances	statements

Academic English

In the article "What Do Business Accountants Do?" you learned that *financial* means "relating to money and other resources." *Financial* can describe things that relate to the money and resources of companies. *Financial* can also describe things that relate to the money and resources of any person, as in the following sentence.

We keep financial records for our family in a drawer at home.

Complete the sentence below.

1. My *financial* decision was that I had enough money to buy _____

Now use the word *financial* in a sentence of your own.

2. _____

_____

You also learned that *specific* means "certain" or "particular." *Specific* can describe particular jobs that accountants do. *Specific* can also describe any certain or particular thing, as in the following sentence.

I like that specific brand of shoes because they are comfortable.

Complete the sentence below.

3. The *specific* toppings I like on my pizza are _____

Now use the word *specific* in two sentences of your own.

4. _____

5. _____

 Share your new sentences with a partner.

Writing a Postcard

Read the postcard. Then complete the sentences. Use words from the Word Bank.

Hello, Julia! I am on the Moon! I am part of a
(1) _____ mission with a (2) _____
goal. We know that the surface of the Moon
(3) _____ of different types of rocks and dust.
We want to find ways that the rocks and dust can help us.
I have created a substance that is (4) _____
from moon rocks. If you put the substance in the gas tank
of your car, your car will use less gas. Who knows what else
we will (5) _____ as we study the Moon? See you
back on Earth!

-Mario

Word Bank

lunar
consists
derived
achieve
specific

Julia Lee
1431 Main Street
Your Town, Your State
12345
U.S.A.
EARTH

Reading an Instant-Messaging Conversation

Read the instant-messaging conversation between Monique and Kiri. Circle the
word that completes each sentence.

INSTA-CHAT

Monique: Hi, Kiri. Did you ask your mom if you could come to my house to work on our science project?

Kiri: I did, but she found one (**solar, minor**) problem with our plan. She needs to work late tonight, so she can't drive me. How about tomorrow?

Monique: I can meet you tomorrow at the library near your house. I'll bring the folder I (**margin, created**) for our project. Can you bring a (**compass, radius**) to draw the circles on our solar system poster?

Kiri: Don't forget that we have to explain the (**method, base**) we used to find information about the solar system.

Monique: You're right. We can use the books at the library. They will be an (**auditor, asset**) to our project. We also can ask the librarians for help.

Kiri: See you after school tomorrow!

Work with a partner. Talk about what the words mean. How can you use the words to talk about Earth? List your ideas in the outline of Earth below.

| galaxy | site | astronomical | principle | financial |
| cycle | tons | circumference | universe | accountants |

Use all of the words above in complete sentences of your own. Each sentence may include one or more of the words. To help you start writing, look at the ideas you wrote about. After you write your sentences, read them over. If you find a mistake, correct it.

_____

_____

_____

_____

_____

_____

Glossary

A

abbreviation (ə brē′vē ā′shən) one or more letters that represent a whole word or phrase [2]

accountants (ə kount′ənts) people who gather and organize information about money [15]

*****achieve** (ə chēv′) to get or do something successfully [12]

adjustments (ə just′mənts) changes that help to reach a goal [6]

aerodynamics (ār′ō dī nam′iks) the science of how objects move through gases [8]

*****affect** (ə fekt′) to make something change [1]

ancient (ān′shənt) related to times that were long ago [9]

*****area** (ār′ē ə) a particular surface, space, or region [4]

arrange (ə rānj′) to put things in a certain order [9]

asset (as′et) money that someone has, or something that is worth money [15]

assumes (ə sōōmz′) considers something to be a fact without knowing it for certain [7]

astronomical (as′trə nom′i kəl) extremely large [14]

astronomy (əs tron′ə mē) the science of outer space [14]

auditors (ô′də tərz) accountants who make sure that financial statements are correct [15]

*****available** (ə vā′lə bəl) ready to have or to use [10]

average (av′rij) the sum of a set of numbers divided by how many numbers are in the set [8]

B

base (bās) the bottom part that supports something that stands on it [12]

budget (buj′it) a plan to use a certain amount of money for a set purpose [6]

C

calendar (kal′ən dər) a way to divide time into set amounts throughout a year [11]

caterers (kā′tər ərz) people who provide food and other services for an event [6]

circumference (sər kum′fər əns) the distance around a circle [13]

coefficient (kō′i fish′ənt) a number that can be used to calculate how much a certain thing changes when its conditions change (the number is different for different things) [8]

compare (kəm pār′) to examine how things are alike and different [5]

comparison (kəm par′ə sən) an examination of how things are alike and different [3]

compass (kum′pəs) an instrument that people use to draw perfect circles [13]

*****compute** (kəm pūt′) to calculate an amount or a number [8]

connected (kə nek′tid) joined or linked together [7]

*****consists** (kən sists′) is made up of different parts or items [14]

*****constructed** (kən strukt′əd) built; put together [9]

*****created** (krē āt′əd) made something; caused something to exist [11]

D

credit (kred′it) trust or confidence that a person can repay a loan or pay a bill [10]

cycle (sī′kəl) a group of events that occur over and over in a certain order [11]

debit (deb′it) an amount of money that has been spent [15]

degrees (di grēz′) steps that add up to measure the amount of something [2]

denominator (di nom′ə nā′tər) the number below the line in a fraction by which the upper number is divided [3]

*****derived** (di rīvd′) traced back to a certain source or starting point [13]

*****design** (di zīn′) to use skills to plan the parts and details of something [8]

detail (dē′tāl) the small features or parts of something [4]

diameter (dī am′ə tər) a straight line that begins at any point on a circle, passes through the center of the circle, and ends on the opposite side of the circle [13]

E

*****establish** (es tab′lish) to show that something exists or is true [7]

event (i vent′) an important thing that occurs; a gathering of people for a purpose [6]

F

*****factors** (fak′tərz) things that cause results or that are important parts in a situation [10]

---

* Academic English word

feature (fē′chər) a part of something [9]

****final** (fīn′əl) last; at the end of something [6]

****financial** (fī nan′shəl) relating to money and other resources [15]

****formula** (fôr′myə lə) a way to find an answer [3]

fraction (frak′shən) a part of a whole shown as a numerator over a denominator [3]

friction (frik′shən) a force that slows down the movement of one surface against another [8]

G

galaxy (gal′ək sē) a group of stars and clouds of gases and dust [14]

gallon (gal′ən) a measurement of a certain amount of a liquid [1]

geometry (jē om′ə trē) the area of mathematics that studies points, lines, and shapes [13]

H

host (hōst) to have a party, meeting, or other event that guests attend [6]

I

inclined planes (in klīnd′ plānz) tilted surfaces that people use to move heavy objects [12]

instrument (in′strə mənt) a device that measures the condition or the work of something [1]

interest (in′trist) money that a customer pays to borrow money from a lender [10]

****involve** (in volv′) to include as an important part [3]

item (ī′təm) something that is part of a larger group or set [5]

L

leap year (lēp yēr) a calendar year with an extra day that occurs every fourth year [11]

lend (lend) to allow someone to use an item and then return it [10]

liability (lī′ə bil′ə tē) money that someone must pay to a person or company [15]

light-year (līt yēr) the distance that light travels through space in one year [14]

****locate** (lō′kāt) to find the exact place or position of something [4]

lunar (loo′nər) having to do with the Moon [11]

M

****maintain** (mān tān′) to keep something in good condition and able to work well [1]

margin (mär′jin) amount or degree of difference [12]

****method** (meth′əd) a way of doing something that helps to reach a goal [11]

mileage (mī′lij) the number of miles a car can travel on a certain amount of gas [1]

****minor** (mī′nər) small in size or amount [14]

mortgage (môr′gij) a loan that people use to buy a house [10]

N

networks (net′wurks′) groups or systems of things that are linked in some way [7]

****normal** (nôr′məl) common or usual [2]

numerals (noo′mər əlz) symbols that represent numbers [9]

O

odometer (ō dom′ə tər) a device in a car that measures how far the car has traveled [1]

P

percentage (pər sen′tij) a part of a whole as it relates to 100 [3]

****principle** (prin′sə pəl) a rule that explains how something works [13]

product (prod′əkt) something that people can buy [5]

profit (prof′it) the money that remains after a business has paid all of its costs [10]

proved (proovd) showed something to be true [7]

****purchase** (pur′chəs) to buy something [5]

pyramid (pir′ə mid′) a structure with a square base and four triangular sides that form a point at the top [12]

Q

quantity (kwon′tə tē) the amount or number of something [5]

R

radius (rā′dē əs) the distance from the center of a circle to a point on the circumference [13]

****range** (rānj) the area between two limits, such as an upper limit and a lower limit [2]

ratio (rā′shē ō′) the relationship between the amount, number, or size of two things [4]

---

* Academic English word

Lesson numbers appear in brackets.

records (rek′ərdz) information that people write down and save [9]

relationship (ri lā′shən ship′) a connection or link between things [4]

representation (rep′ri zen tā′shən) something that looks like or stands for something else [4]

S

scale (skāl) the relationship between sizes on a map and sizes on Earth's surface [4]

scales (skālz) ways to measure things based on a certain series of steps [2]

*selection (si lek′shən) a group of things to choose from [6]

separation (sep′ə rā′shən) distance or gap between two things [7]

*site (sīt) the place where something is, was, or will be [12]

solar (sō′lər) having to do with the Sun [11]

*specific (spi sif′ik) certain; particular [15]

speedometer (spē dom′ə tər) a device that measures how fast a car is traveling [1]

symbol (sim′bəl) a letter or shape that represents something [3]

system (sis′təm) a group of things that combine to form one larger group or whole [9]

T

temperature (tem′prə chər) a measurement of how hot or cold something is [2]

*theory (thē′ər ē) an idea that may be true but that no one has showed to be true [7]

thermometer (thər mom′ə tər) a device that measures temperature [2]

tons (tunz) units of weight equal to about 2,000 pounds [12]

U

units (ū′nits) specific amounts that people use to measure the quantity of something [5]

universe (ū′nə vurs′) everything that exists in space, including the stars and the planets [14]

V

value (val′ū) a good price for the quality and amount of an item or service [5]

velocity (vi los′ə tē) the rate at which something moves in a certain direction [8]

---

* Academic English word

Personal Dictionary